Celtic

IT'S NOT TRIVIA, IT'S MORE IMPORTANT THAN THAT

ROUGH GUIDE

11s

Written by
Steve Morgan

Text editors
Paul Simpson, Helen Rodiss,
Michaela Bushell

Production
Ian Cranna, Tim Oldham,
Andy Pringle, Tim Harrison,
Ann Oliver

Cover and book design
Sharon O'Connor

Cover image
Charlie Best

Thanks to: Jim Kerr,
Gerry Lowe, Ian McLeish, Mark
Benstead, Joe Gilhooley, Simon
Cairns, Thomas McGuigan, and
Jo, Jack and Holly

Printed in Spain
by Graphy Cems

This edition published
July 2005 was prepared by
Haymarket Network for
Rough Guides Ltd,
80 Strand, London, WC2R ORL

Distributed by the
Penguin Group
Penguin Books Ltd,
27 Wrights Lane,
London W8 5TZ

A catalogue record for this
book is available from the
British Library

ISBN 1-84353-565-3

ROUGH
GUIDES

Contents

ROUGH GUIDE
11s
Celtic

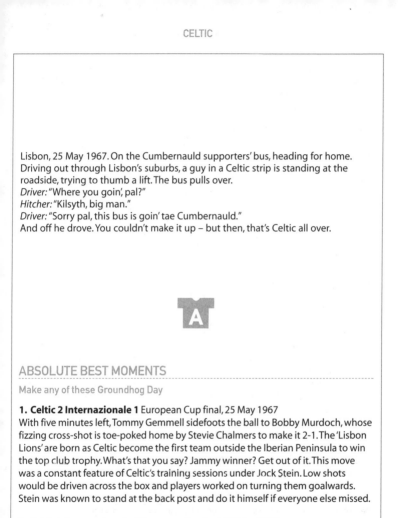

Lisbon, 25 May 1967. On the Cumbernauld supporters' bus, heading for home.
Driving out through Lisbon's suburbs, a guy in a Celtic strip is standing at the
roadside, trying to thumb a lift. The bus pulls over.
Driver: "Where you goin', pal?"
Hitcher: "Kilsyth, big man."
Driver: "Sorry pal, this bus is goin' tae Cumbernauld."
And off he drove. You couldn't make it up – but then, that's Celtic all over.

ABSOLUTE BEST MOMENTS

Make any of these Groundhog Day

1. Celtic 2 Internazionale 1 European Cup final, 25 May 1967
With five minutes left, Tommy Gemmell sidefoots the ball to Bobby Murdoch, whose
fizzing cross-shot is toe-poked home by Stevie Chalmers to make it 2-1. The 'Lisbon
Lions' are born as Celtic become the first team outside the Iberian Peninsula to win
the top club trophy. What's that you say? Jammy winner? Get out of it. This move
was a constant feature of Celtic's training sessions under Jock Stein. Low shots
would be driven across the box and players worked on turning them goalwards.
Stein was known to stand at the back post and do it himself if everyone else missed.

2. Celtic 2 Internazionale 1 European Cup final, 25 May 1967
Same golden game. Different golden moment. With 63 minutes gone, Inter lead 1-0.
Jim Craig, transgressor for the Italians' seventh-minute penalty, cuts the ball back on
the edge of the area. Tommy Gemmell has timed a foraging run to perfection and

his piledriver flashes past Giuliano Sarti at 70mph to make the score 1-1. Game on. Around 12,000 sunburned Celts in the ground start to believe the impossible. All the talk before the game had been about whether the Bhoys could bear the early evening heat of Lisbon: now it was Inter's turn to look hot and sweaty…

3. Celtic 4 Rangers 2 21 May 1979
Crunch time, final game of the season. Celtic top, Rangers are three points behind but with two games in hand. Seven minutes remain and it's 2-2: a point puts Rangers in the driving seat for a second successive Treble. Celtic, incidentally, have been playing with ten men since Johnny Doyle was dismissed 35 minutes in for taking a kick at Alex McDonald. Then it happens. Peter McCloy pushes George McCluskey's cross out, but only as far as Colin Jackson, who deflects it into his own net for 3-2. Jackson says to Bobby Lennox: "I'd hate to be remembered as the man who lost the league for Rangers." Don't you fret, son. A Murdo MacLeod screamer from 20 yards makes it 4-2 and there's barely time for the match to restart. Billy McNeill, in his first season, follows Jock Stein into the history books as captain and manager of a Celtic title-winning team. "There's a fairytale aspect of Celtic which shows itself every now and again," he said. "That was another of our wee tales which will be remembered as long as anyone is alive who was there to see it. Even our European Cup win in 1967 wasn't as emotionally demanding or exhausting."

4. Celtic 7 Rangers 1 Scottish League Cup final, 19 October 1957
"Oh, Hampden in the sun, Celtic 7 Rangers 1." It's still the biggest winning margin in a British cup final and unlikely to be beaten any time soon. Joy unconfined, with Billy McPhail's hat-trick goal the icing on the cake as he heads the ball past Rangers centre-back Valentine before beating Niven. A shower of bottles rains down from the Rangers end as Willie Fernie tucks away a last-minute penalty to make it seventh heaven. If only their team had shown some bottle in the previous 89 minutes. After the match, a fan asks Celtic's Charlie Tully the time. He responds: "The only time I know is seven past Niven." Quality.

5. Celtic 2 St Johnstone 0 8 May 1998
Victory would ensure the title for the Bhoys, anything less a footballing apocalypse: ten straight Rangers title triumphs. Goals from Harald Brattbakk and Henrik Larsson mean 'cheerio ten in a row'. Of course, the title should have been sewn up long before the last day, but the significance of the victory is everything.

6. Celtic 6 Rangers 2 27 August 2000
Martin O'Neill's first Old Firm game – or the 'Demolition Derby' to give it its correct name. Chris Sutton's 51st-second opener – the fastest Old Firm goal in history

(Sutton has improved on it since) – lays down the marker, and it's 3-0 inside 12 minutes through Stilian Petrov and Paul Lambert. All well and good. But it's the wonder goal from Henrik Larsson that really burns the retinas. The Swede breaks free, nutmegging Bert Konterman before exquisitely chipping Stefan Klos to make it 4-1. Dreamland. On a day like today, even Bobby Petta can look good. O'Neill's Treble year was pretty special, but the jigsaw's nothing without the first piece in place.

7. Celtic 2 Dundee United 1 Scottish Cup final, 14 May 1988

Kevin Gallacher – grandson of Patsy – does his best to poop Celtic's centenary Double party by leaving Roy Aitken for dead to score the opening goal in the blinding Hampden sun. Champagne remains firmly on ice until the last quarter of an hour, when Frank McAvennie evens things up by heading home Anton Rogan's cross. With seconds left, Joe Miller sclaffs his corner and Billy Stark's shot falls kindly after bouncing off David Narey's shin. United keeper Billy Thomson is wrong-footed, McAvennie must score. He does. An unforgettable end to an unforgettable season.

8. Celtic 3 Dunfermline 1 Scottish League Cup final, 22 May 2004

All good things must come to an end. In this case it's Henrik Larsson's Celtic career, but what a curtain call. With 32 minutes to go, at 1-0 down Celtic are a bit below Pars, who are rightly enjoying their biggest domestic big day out for 36 years. Picking up Sutton's knockdown from a Pars corner, Larsson has only one thing in mind. Bombing down the left flank, he cuts in to unleash an unstoppable shot past Derek Stillie for his 40th goal of the season. Thirteen minutes later, he bags his 242nd and final goal for the Hoops. Stilian Petrov gets a third in injury time.

9. Celtic 3 Dunfermline 2 Scottish Cup final, 24 April 1965

Jock Stein's first final with Celtic, just a month after officially taking over, was proving tough going. Playing into the teeth of a gale against a team Stein had not long left, Bertie Auld hauled us back twice in a thrilling spectacle, but time was ticking away. Something special was required. That something was Billy McNeill, breaking his goalscoring duck for the season. McNeill's forehead crashed Charlie Gallagher's corner home with nine minutes left to clinch the Hoops' first trophy for eight years. A winning habit that would prove very hard to break had just begun in some style. "It wouldn't have gone as well for Celtic had they not won this game," reflected Stein.

10. Celtic 6 Hibernian 1 Scottish Cup final, 6 May 1972

The blow of a spot-kick defeat by Milan in the European Cup semi-final two weeks earlier is softened by hitting Eddie Turnbull's 'Tornados' for six at Hampden. Billy McNeill gets the ball rolling in true captain's style after just two minutes. Hibs equalise, Celtic go ahead through Dixie Deans, but it's Dixie's second goal after the break that has everyone talking. After Hibs' keeper Jim Herriot makes a hash of his clearance, Deans rounds the hapless Hibee to head for goal along the touchline. He evades the attentions of Brownlie and Herriot again to shoot into an empty net. But it's the somersault that follows that's the best bit. As Hibs crumble, Deans gets another to complete his hat-trick and join Celtic's Jimmy Quinn as only the second player to achieve the feat at the final stage. Lou Macari gets two in the last ten minutes. Ladies and gentlemen, please be upstanding for the biggest Scottish Cup final margin of victory in the 20th century.

11. Celtic 5 Queen's Park 1 Scottish Cup final, 9 April 1892
The problem with half the lists these days is that there's no sense of perspective. So let's redress the balance. This replay saw an imperious Willie Maley marshal his troops superbly to come from a goal down. Celtic had led a snowbound first encounter 1-0 four weeks earlier, but the match had to be played out as a friendly because of regular crowd incursions. Two goals apiece from Johnny Campbell and Sandy McMahon, plus a Sellars own goal, meant a trophy cabinet had to be ordered pronto. Hail, hail, the Celts are here...

> "HAIL, HAIL, THE CELTS ARE HERE..." COULD BE HEARD FOLLOWING THE HOOPS' WIN OVER QUEEN'S PARK

ALL-IRISH XI

Imports from the Emerald Isle

1. **Pat Bonner** born Burtonport, Co Donegal, 1978-94, 1994-95
2. **Paul Byrne** born Dublin, 1993-95
3. **William Cook** born Coleraine, 1930-32
4. **Willie Crone** born Dublin, 1913-14
5. **Sean Fallon** born Sligo, 1950-58
6. **Patsy Gallacher** born Milford, Co Donegal, 1911-26
7. **Neil Lennon** born Lurgan, 2000-
8. **Willie Maley** born Newry, 1888-97
9. **Bertie Peacock** born Coleraine, 1949-61
10. **Anton Rogan** born Belfast, 1986-91
11. **Charlie Tulley** born Belfast, 1948-59

ALL-TIME APPEARANCES (ALL COMPETITIONS)

The most loyal servants

1. **Billy McNeill** 790 (1957-75)
2. **Paul McStay** 677 (1981-97)
3. **Roy Aitken** 672 (1972-90)
4. **Danny McGrain** 663 (1967-87)
5. **Pat Bonner** 641 (1978-94)
6. **Alec McNair** 604 (1904-25)
7. **Bobby Lennox** 589 (1961-80)
8. **Bobby Evans** 535 (1944-60)
9. **Jimmy Johnstone** 515 (1961-75)
   Jimmy McMenemy 515 (1902-20)
11. **Tommy Burns** 508 (1973-89)

ALL-TIME APPEARANCES (LEAGUE)

Saturday after Saturday after Saturday

1. **Alec McNair** 548 (1904-25)
2. **Paul McStay** 515 (1981-97)
3. **Billy McNeill** 486 (1957-75)
4. **Roy Aitken** 483 (1972-90)
   Pat Bonner 483 (1978-94)
6. **Jimmy McMenemy** 456 (1902-20)
7. **Danny McGrain** 441 (1967-87)
8. **Patsy Gallacher** 432 (1911-26)
9. **Charlie Shaw** 420 (1913-25)
10. **Jimmy McStay** 409 (1920-34)
11. **Willie McStay** 399 (1912-29)

ALL-TIME GOALSCORERS (ALL COMPETITIONS)

The greatest marksmen

1. **Jimmy McGrory** 468
2. **Bobby Lennox** 273
3. **Henrik Larsson** 242

4. **Stevie Chalmers** 219
5. **Jimmy Quinn** 217
6. **Patsy Gallacher** 192
7. **John Hughes** 188
8. **Sandy McMahon** 177
9. **Jimmy McMenemy** 168
10. **Kenny Dalglish** 167
11. **Adam McLean** 148

ALL-TIME GOALSCORERS (LEAGUE)

On target week in, week out

1. **Jimmy McGrory** 395
2. **Jimmy Quinn** 187
3. **Patsy Gallacher** 186
4. **Henrik Larsson** 173
5. **Bobby Lennox** 167
6. **Stevie Chalmers** 147
7. **Jimmy McMenemy** 144
8. **Sandy McMahon** 130
9. **Adam McLean** 128
10. **Jimmy McColl** 117
11. **John Hughes** 115

ANAGRAMS XI (1)

Satanic pigs and biting ponces

1. **Packie Bonner** Break-in ponce
2. **Danny McGrain** Can grind many
3. **Alan Stubbs** Satan blubs
4. **Gary Gillespie** Silly eager pig
5. **Olivier Tebily** Oily evil biter
6. **Murdo MacLeod** A more cold mud
7. **Kenny Dalglish** Handy, sell King
8. **Lubomir Moravcik** Club roar I'm vim, OK/I'm a crook, bum rival
9. **Henrik Larsson** No snarl, shriek

10. Chris Sutton Ostrich nuts
11. Bertie Auld Ideal brute

Manager: Jock Stein – Injects KO

ANAGRAMS XI (2)

Grave boobs and clever rats

1. Ronnie Simpson Minor pensions
2. Ramon Vega Grave moan
3. Stilian Petrov Plaintive sort
4. Gianbobo Balde Genial bad boob
5. Andreas Thom Handsome rat
6. Martin Hayes Hysteria man
7. Jimmy Johnstone Hmm, enjoys joint
8. Stevie Chalmers Cleverish mates
9. Pierre van Hooijdonk I jerk on a honored VIP
10. Mo Johnston John Thomson
11. Frank McAvennie Craven knifeman

Manager: Martin O'Neill I'll not remain

> "I'VE SEEN MORE MEAT ON A BUTCHER'S PENCIL" WAS ONE WRITER'S VIEW OF PETER GRANT

ANGRY YOUNG MEN

11 Celtic hotheads

1. Bertie Auld
Bertie refused to leave the pitch after being dismissed in the World Club Championship of 1967. Repeated run-ins with referees earlier in his Celtic career had led to him being shipped out to Birmingham City in 1961. He was also sent off in the friendly against Real Madrid in June 1967.

2. Peter Grant
"I've seen more meat on a butcher's pencil, but he got stuck in and wasn't slow at lambasting more experienced colleagues." So ran one press notice for Grant's showing against Hibs in April 1984. Fearsomely competitive, he was a favourite in the Double-winning season of 1987/88, appearing on crutches to take the

applause after the final game against Dundee. A real jersey player – his celebration of Rangers's own goal in front of the Broomloan during the 2-2 draw at Castle Greyskull that season lives long in the memory. Great at shouting and pointing.

3. Paddy Crerand
An alleged headbutt on national service with Scotland, two scraps against Falkirk in 1961 (the second resulting in a week's suspension by the SFA), as well as a four-week suspension and a wage-stoppage by Bob Kelly. Paddy also played his part in a free-for-all for the national side against Uruguay in May 1962. Eventually fell out with Sean Fallon after a poor first-half against Rangers on New Year's Day 1963, and was transferred to Manchester United at the end of that month. He's still there as a pundit on the Mancs' own MUTV.

4. George Connelly
Numerous walkouts and extended absences wrecked his career as he walked out on the Scottish squad at Berne airport in 1973. Never the same player after David Hay left for Chelsea, he threatened to quit there and then but was persuaded otherwise by Stein. He won four titles and was an exquisite passer of the ball. But the 1973 Footballer of the Year had given up the game by 1976, just eight years after making his debut. A sad tale.

5. Jimmy Quinn
Celtic's legendary striker between 1900-15 was dismissed twice against Rangers, first in 1905, for trampling on Alec Craig, and again in 1907, for supposedly kicking Joe Henry. Both offences were followed by long suspensions.

6. Paolo Di Canio
"Paolo often storms off the training pitch in the middle of a game if something doesn't go right. Maybe it's the Italian way, or more likely he is a nutter." West Ham's Neil Ruddock learns what we'd all known for a while in 1999. The Mussolini-loving Di Canio played his trump lunatic hand in England, shoving referee Paul Allcock while playing for Sheffield Wednesday.

7. Dariuz Dziekanowski
Not so mad on the pitch – boss Billy McNeill described him as "a magnificent trainer" – but the 'George Best of Poland' tag wasn't earned for his quiet nights in.

8. Johnny Doyle
Conversely, a terrible trainer, but certainly more mad. Doyle watched from the dugout in one of the club's finest hours, May 1979's 4-2 title-clincher, having been

sent off for kicking Alex McDonald. Great style for a cult hero, perhaps, but minus several million points for common sense.

9. Bobby Collins
'The Wee Barra' stood just 5ft 4in tall, but he was someone you tangled with at your peril. His Govanhill youth had taught him well, but an over-enthusiastic challenge on the Clyde keeper in 1955's Scottish Cup final saw him dropped for the replay.

10. Martin O'Neill
Remonstrated with fans barracking Neil Lennon for passing the ball back to Rab Douglas with the score 1-1 during the UEFA Cup semi-final clash with Boavista at Parkhead. When the culprits had a go back, John Robertson had to usher his furious boss away.

11. Jimmy Johnstone
After being substituted against Dundee United in 1968 for failing to obey Jock Stein's tactics, Jinky was suspended for a week following a row with his boss in the tunnel. Stein had pursued him there for an apology after a series of gestures and abuse. Johnstone ruled himself out of a starting place in Scotland's 1974 World Cup side after flicking the Vs at the press box in the team's final preparation match.

Sub: Dixie Deans Only warrants a place on the bench because of his initial promise – he arrived from Motherwell in 1971 in the middle of a six-week ban – but settled down to become a good Bhoy and was dismissed just once, for the reserves in 1975.

ANNIVERSARIES WORTH NOTING

11 excuses for a nip

1. 10 March 1965
Jock Stein's first game in charge. Airdrie get a 6-0 pasting on their own patch.

2. 20 April 1907
A first domestic Double, beating Hearts 3-0 at Hampden Park in the Scottish Cup final with goals from Peter Somers (2) and Willie Orr.

3. 24 April 1965
Jock Stein's new charges beat his old ones (Dunfermline Athletic) to win the Scottish Cup. A new era starts here.

4. 14 May 1988
Frank McAvennie's late, late winner in the Scottish Cup final against Dundee United at Hampden secures a centenary Double.

5. 25 May 1967
The Lisbon Lions roar in Celtic's finest hour. Treat yourself to a nice day off. Why not recreate Tommy Gemmell's goal in your back yard? Mind the windows.

6. 28 May 1888
The first official match for the newly founded Celtic FC. A friendly meeting with yes, you guessed it, Rangers, ends in a 5-2 victory. Fancy that.

7. 15 August 1903
The Bhoys wear green-and-white hoops for the first time in a 2-1 victory over Partick Thistle at Celtic Park.

8. 26 September 1962
First encounter against European opposition – a 4-2 defeat in Valencia in the Inter-Cities Fairs Cup (predecessor of the current UEFA Cup).

9. 12 October 1959
First floodlit match played at Celtic Park – a 2-0 defeat in a friendly against Wolves.

10. 22 October 1922
Jock Stein born on this day.

11. 6 November 1887
John Glass chairs the meeting at the parish hall of St Mary's, East Rose Street, Glasgow, at which Celtic Football Club is founded.

BALLS OF STEEL
Real men, doing real men's things

1. Big Willie style
Willie Maley stands up to the striking trio of Barney Battles, John Divers and Charlie Meechan, who refuse to play against Hibs in November 1896 following critical press reports of the club's aggressive style. The trio are ousted; Maley becomes secretary-manager – the club's first – in April 1897 and wins the title in his first full season in the job in 1897/98. He serves for the next 40 years, his tenure characterised by an iron will and strict discipline. You don't say.

2. Way to go, Joe
Joe Cassidy, out for just three weeks with a broken jaw suffered against Rangers, returns to lead the forward line in the 1923 Scottish Cup final against Hibs and scores the only goal.

3. Canny Kenny
It's 14 August 1971. Ken Dalglish, as he's called in the *Glasgow Times* the next day, is making his Old Firm debut at Ibrox against the team he supported as a boy. Celtic, already a goal up, are awarded a spot-kick. Dalglish volunteers his services. You'd think he might be nervous with the small matter of 72,000 in the ground, most of whom are willing him to miss. What is he doing? He's stopping to tie his bloody laces properly first. He's 20 years old. A star is born.

4. Danny Bhoy
A fractured skull in 1972, diagnosed with diabetes in 1974, an ankle injury that cost him 18 months of his career in 1977… but Danny McGrain still kept coming back for more. Six league championships make him Celtic's second most-decorated title winner behind Billy McNeill, four of these as skipper.

5. From a Jock to a king

Jock Stein wins a tense game of brinkmanship with the Celtic directors in March 1965. They give him the manager's post full-time – at the third time of asking. Stein has refused to become assistant boss to, and then joint manager with, Sean Fallon. He is within a whisker of moving to Wolves until Robert Kelly finally does the right thing and gives in. Good call.

6. King of (S)pain – Jimmy Johnstone rules, OK

"He was provoked, he refused to retaliate, he showed tremendous restraint. I'm proud of him." Sometimes you've got to fight when you're a man. But enough Kenny Rogers, more Kipling. It's also a skill to keep your head when all about you are losing theirs. That's what Jinky did against the 'animals' of Atletico Madrid in the European Cup quarter-final first leg of April 1974. Atletico ended the match with eight men – and a goalless draw. To the spoilers, the victory, unfortunately. Celtic lost the away leg 2-0 after death threats were made to Stein and Johnstone before the match.

7. Sling when you're winning

Sean Fallon returns with a cracked collarbone – and his arm in a sling – to complete the match against Hearts in the 1953/54 Double-winning season. "It wasn't as if it was a broken leg!" he scoffs.

8. In the line of fire

The defence in front of him wasn't all that clever, but Willie Miller's bravery between the sticks between 1942-50 was something else. His stitches count was in three figures for his head alone – extraordinarily courageous given that Celtic keeper John Thomson's death from head injuries had cast such a shadow at Parkhead.

9. On your way, son

Imagine, just for the heck of it, that you are Jock Stein. It's the spring of 1971, and John Hughes, a stalwart of your great late-1960s side, asks you for a pay rise. What do you do? You remind him that it's his fault Celtic lost the 1970 European Cup final and promptly ship him off to Crystal Palace.

10. The party's over

Jock Stein calls time on the Lisbon Lions on the day of the championship-clinching win over Ayr United. He announces that the final game of the 1970/71 season, against Clyde, will be the last chance to see his team in action. Bobby Lennox's hat-trick is the icing on the cake in a 6-1 win. You've got to quit while you're ahead. And Celtic stay ahead in 1971/72, winning the league by ten points from their nearest challengers Aberdeen, including a 27-match unbeaten sequence.

11. Bloody marvel

John Clark, nostrils plugged with cotton wool, continues playing in his blood-stained shirt as Celtic defeat Dunfermline Athletic to give Jock Stein his first trophy, the 1965 Scottish Cup.

BEST AWAY DAYS

11 biggest wins on the road

1. **9-1 v Arbroath** League Cup, 25 August 1993
2. **8-0 v Dumbarton** League Cup, 23 August 1975
   8-0 v Hamilton Academical 5 November 1988
4. **8-1 v Cowdenbeath** League Cup, 17 September 1958
   8-1 v Raith Rovers League Cup, 15 September 1965
   8-1 v Dundee 16 January 1971
7. **7-0 v St Mirren** 3 November 1962
   7-0 v Clyde 1 January 1972
   7-0 v Motherwell 18 September 1982
   7-0 v Berwick Rangers League Cup, 9 August 1997
   7-0 v Arthurlie Scottish Cup, 8 January 1898

BHOY SELECTORS!

11 players who've managed English clubs

1. **Billy McNeill** Manchester City, Aston Villa
2. **Jimmy Sirrel** Brentford, Notts County, Sheffield United
3. **David Moyes** Bristol City, Preston North End, Everton
4. **Tommy Docherty** Aston Villa, Manchester United, QPR
5. **Mick McCarthy** Barnsley, Sunderland
6. **Kenny Dalglish** Liverpool, Blackburn Rovers, Newcastle United
7. **Scott Duncan** Manchester United
8. **Bobby Murdoch** Middlesbrough
9. **Lou Macari** Swindon Town, West Ham United, Birmingham City, Stoke City
10. **Tommy Burns** Reading
11. **John Gorman** Swindon Town

BIG MACS XI

We're loving 'em

1. Dan McArthur
2. Danny McGrain
3. Jackie McNamara
4. Billy McNeill
5. Roddie McDonald
6. Jimmy McMenemy
7. Paul McStay
8. Murdo MacLeod
9. Jimmy McGrory
10. Frank McGarvey
11. George McCluskey

BIG MAN ON CAMPUS

11 great Jock Stein quotes

1. *"You need four men at the back who can tackle, four in midfield who can pass the ball, and two up front who have pace and can shoot. Then, as long as the balance is right between right-sided and left-sided players, you've got a team."*
Stein makes the essence of team-building sound surprisingly simple – clearly not too fussed about goalkeepers, however.

2. *"It is up to us, to everyone at Celtic Park, to build our own legends. We don't want to live with history, to be compared with legends from the past. We must make new legends."*
Stein gets ready to kick on after his first title, May 1966.

3. *"Next season we will be in the European Cup for the first time. This is the biggest tournament but I don't think the boys have anything to be afraid of."*
Stein draws up the battle plans…

4. *"I feel we have the players fit to wear the mantle of champions of Europe, I have told them so. Now we know it's up to them."*
The Big Man bigs up the Bhoys before the quarter-final against Vojvodina Novi Sad, March 1967.

5. *"I wonder how many months' overtime those lads have put in to be here tonight?"*
Stein delivers a top pep talk to his players as they take to the pitch in Lisbon for the pre-match walkabout.

6. *"Is he better in midfield or up front? Och, just let him out on the park."*
Stein on where to play Kenny Dalglish.

7. *"He's not a bad boy with regard to being against authority. It is just that if there is trouble, or a problem, Jimmy (Johnstone) always seems to be in the thick of it."*
Jock on Jinky.

8. *"Play to your strengths and disguise your weaknesses."*

9. *"The best place to defend is in the other team's penalty box."*

10. *"A circus act."*
Stein vents his spleen on penalty shoot-outs in the wake of European Cup semi-final exit to Milan in 1972.

11. *"They've got half-a-dozen Argentinians in their pool and the manager's one, so that means a riot for a start."*
Stein's one step ahead of the game on hearing of European Cup pairing with Atletico Madrid in 1974.

THE BOY'S A BIT SPECIAL

11 opponents we wish had played for us

1. Alfredo Di Stefano
A 76,000 all-ticket crowd packed out Parkhead for a friendly against Real Madrid on 10 September 1962, two weeks before Celtic's debut European tie against Valencia. Madrid win 3-1 and give the Celtic players tartan travel rugs as souvenirs. Cheers!

2. Ronaldinho
What a great Bhoy from Brazil the Barça star would make. After Rafael Scheidt, surely it's the least the Hoops deserve…

3. Johan Cruyff
Scourge of the Hoops' defence in a 3-0 battering in Amsterdam in the 1970/71

European Cup quarter-finals, and also seen again in 1982/83, when we won. Cruyff, by now 35, turned out in the memorable night at Celtic Park, giving away a penalty for a foul on Tommy Burns in a 2-2 draw. We liked him even more when he said: "For Celtic I like the red-haired man." That'll be Tommy Burns.

4. John Greig MBE
You've got to respect that kind of durability. A real hard man, too.

5. Davie Cooper
A constant menace to right-backs down the years. The game was poorer for his passing at the ridiculously young age of 39. RIP.

6. Willie Henderson
The Gers' equivalent of Jimmy Johnstone. Only half as good, and without a European Cup winner's medal.

7. Jim Baxter
A real show pony, but a damn fine one with it. One of the sweetest left feet the Scottish game has seen. RIP.

8. Andy Goram
Yes he's a dick, but you have to say he was a pretty decent keeper too.

9. Dynamo Kiev
Valeri Lobanovski's squad contained 14 of the Russian national pool. They did for us 4-2 on aggregate in the 1986/87 European Cup, but they were worth watching.

10. Vojvodina Novi Sad
Clever Yugoslavs were a tough barrier to overcome on the path to Lisbon – it took a Billy McNeill goal in the last minute to put them out.

11. Ally McCoist
Cocky as they come and a real pain in the arse, but has there been a better recent Scottish striker?

YES. ANDY GORAM IS A DICK. BUT YOU HAVE TO SAY HE WAS A PRETTY DECENT KEEPER TOO

BREAKING THE BANK

11 big-money signings. You decide who gave best value

1. **Ronnie Glavin** Partick Thistle, November 1974 (£80,000)
2. **Davie Provan** Kilmarnock, September 1978 (£120,000)
3. **Frank McGarvey** Liverpool, March 1980 (£325,000)
4. **Mo Johnston** Watford, October 1984 (£400,000)
5. **Mick McCarthy** Manchester City, May 1987 (£425,000)
6. **Tony Cascarino** Aston Villa, July 1991 (£1.1 million)
7. **Stuart Slater** West Ham United, August 1992 (£1.5 million)
8. **Phil O'Donnell** Motherwell, September 1994 (£1.75 million)
9. **Andreas Thom** Bayer Leverkusen, July 1995 (£2.2 million)
10. **Eyal Berkovic** West Ham United, July 1999 (£5.75 million)
11. **Chris Sutton** Chelsea, July 2000 (£6 million)

BRIEF ENCOUNTERS

11 Scottish Cup opponents we'll probably never meet again

1. **6th G.R.V.** 1898/99 (W 8-1)
2. **Thornliebank** 1901/02 (W 3-0)
3. **Leith Athletic** 1908/09 (W 4-2)
4. **Galston** 1910/11 (W 1-0)
5. **Solway Star** 1924/25 (W 2-0)
6. **Dalbeattie Star** 1933/34 (W 6-0)
7. **Nithsdale Wanderers** 1937/38 (W 5-0)
8. **Burntisland Shipyard Amateurs** 1938/39 (W 8-3)
9. **Duns** 1950/51 (W 4-0)
10. **Eyemouth United** 1952/53 (W 4-0) and 1963/64 (W 3-0)
11. **Forres Mechanics** 1956/57 (W 5-0)

BROTHERS IN ARMS

11 Celtic siblings

1. Frank and Jim Brogan
2. James and John Devlin
3. Frank and Mick Dolan

4. Mick and Tom Dunbar
5. Thomas and William Lyon
6. Tom and Willie Maley
7. George and John McCluskey
8. John and Billy McPhail
9. Willie and Jimmy McStay
10. Paul and Willie McStay
11. Frank and Hugh O'Donnell

CAN WE PLAY YOU EVERY WEEK?

Superb thrashings of Clyde. (Bully Wee? More like we bully…)

1. 9-1 25 December 1897
   9-1 4 September 1971
3. 9-2 Scottish Cup, 8 December 1898
4. 7-0 15 January 1927
   7-0 1 January 1972
6. 7-1 26 December 1953
7. 7-2 29 August 1891
   7-2 17 August 1896
9. 6-0 29 January 1938
10. 6-1 25 September 1897
    6-1 27 February 1961
    6-1 1 May 1971

CAPTAIN MARVELS

Celtic's most successful skippers

1. Billy McNeill nine league championships, one European Cup, seven Scottish Cups, six League Cups

2. **Danny McGrain** four league championships
3. **Willie Orr** three league championships, two Scottish Cups
4. **Jimmy Hay** three league championships, two Scottish Cups
5. **Jim Young** three league championships, two Scottish Cups
6. **James Kelly** three league championships, one Scottish Cup
7. **Willie Cringan** two league championships, one Scottish Cup
8. **Willie Lyon** two league championships, one Scottish Cup
9. **Tom Boyd** two league championships, one Scottish Cup, three League Cups
10. **Paul Lambert** two league championships, one Scottish Cup
11. **Willie McStay** one league championship, two Scottish Cups

CELEBRITY CELTS

Don't I know you? Familiar faces in the stands

1. Ardal O'Hanlon
Father Ted's simpleton sidekick was smart enough to pick the Hoops as his team, though he seems to have an interest in Leeds United, too.

2. John Higgins
Snooker loopy he may be, but he's also Hoopy loopy.

3. Billy Connolly
The Big Yin has his own seat at Celtic Park, even if he's rarely in it.

4. Del Amitri
MOR outfit who also penned the official World Cup 1998 anthem. *Nothing Ever Happens* clearly wasn't written for us.

5. Clare Grogan
Gregory's Girl cutie and helium-tonsilled former Altered Images star.

6. Fran Healy
Travis singer has declared his affections for the Hoops, though schoolboy photos exist of him in a Nottingham Forest shirt.

7. Roy Keane
Claims he supported Spurs as a kid, but we all know that's baloney.

8. Jim Kerr
Simple Minds frontman, probably not on Fergus McCann's Christmas card list for his outspoken views on his tenure at Parkhead.

9. Shane McGowan
Gap-toothed Pogues frontman.

10. Teenage Fanclub
Evergreen indie act from Bellshill, home of Billy McNeill.

11. Rod Stewart
Rod the Mod immortalised the Bhoys in song in *You're In My Heart*.

Sub: Pope John Paul II Well, it's always handy to have God on your side.

CELEBRITY CELTS 2

Other famous personages alleged, with varying degrees of plausibility, to have a liking for the Bhoys

1. Bono
Jim Kerr insists the U2 icon is a Celtic fan, so who are we to argue?

2. Frank Carson

3. Bill Gates
Once mentioned as a potential bidder in an unlikely consortium which also involved Kenny Dalglish.

4. Damien Duff
Allegedly arranged Celtic singalongs on the Blackburn Rovers team bus. Such frenetic energy conflicts with reports that all he ever does on a team bus is sleep.

5. Mark Hughes
Publicly praised Celtic fans – a statement in no way connected to the fact that he had a testimonial against the Bhoys in the offing.

6. Eddie Jordan
Allegedly in cahoots with Mr Microsoft and King Kenny…

11. CENTENARY DOUBLE-WINNERS

Packie Bonner

Chris Morris　　　　　　　　　Anton Rogan
　　　Mick McCarthy　　Derek Whyte
　　　　　　　　　(Billy Stark)

Joe Miller　Roy Aitken　Paul McStay　Tommy Burns

　Frank McAvennie　　　　　Andy Walker
　　　　　　　　　　　　(Mark McGhee)

The Celtic team that beat Dundee United 2-1 at Hampden Park on 14 May 1988 to lift the Scottish Cup and record a memorable Double in the club's centenary year.

7. Gary Kelly
A phantom season-ticket holder.

8. David O'Leary
Outed on the grounds that a) he's Irish and b) he played alongside Charlie Nicholas.

9. Jimmy Nail
Only turns up at Celtic Park when we play Newcastle – coincidence?

10. Ian Rush
There is some part of Rushie that will be forever green and white, allegedly.

11. Westlife
It could be worse… it could be S Club 7.

CELTIC GO POP

11 musical moments of varying quality…

1. Road To Paradise
Shane McGowan. Pogues frontman and Hoops fancier teams up with Busted/
Westlife singer-songwriter John McLaughlin for charity single in aid of motor
neurone disease, from which Jimmy Johnstone suffers. The B-side is…

2. Dirty Ol' Town
Jim Kerr and Jimmy Johnstone rework Ewan McColl's classic folk song. According
to fellow conspirator Shane McGowan, Jinky is a better singer than Jim Kerr!

> CALEY GRABBED A
> THIRD AND YOU KNOW
> NEXT DAY'S HEADLINE.
> BY THE END OF THE DAY,
> BARNES WAS GONE

3. You're In My Heart
Rod Stewart immortalises the Hoops in song in
1974. "You're Celtic, United, but baby, I've decided
you're the best team I've ever seen." Ooh, go on
then, you old smoothie.

4. Celtic Celtic
The Celtic Squad of 1967. Celebrating winning
everything by singing in that bad way that only
footballers can.

5. Celtic, Your Favourites In Green
The Celtic Squad. A 1973 single on Polydor. Don't all rush at once.

6. The Celtic Rap: Boot Mix
The Celtic Squad 1988 (Scratch Records). Next…

7. The Celtic Song: If We Only Had Old Ireland Over Here
John Daly, 1961. The B-side was *We Don't Care If We Win, Lose or Draw*. Hmm….

8. Passing Time
Jimmy Johnstone, featured on *Second Celtic Songs* EP (GD Records). A romantic
ballad, originally the B-side of 1970's *Celtic Are Here* single.

9. Best Days Of Our Lives
John McLaughlin again. This tribute to the Lisbon Lions comes complete with
a spooky Martin O'Neill voiceover which sounds like it was done in a cave.

10. Her Hooped Dream
Clare Grogan. If you liked Altered Images, don't listen to this. From *The Ultimate Celtic Album*, also featuring Rod Stewart, Frankie Miller, Shane McGowan, James Grant and various lesser lights (Concept Music – £14.99, of which £1 goes to charity).

11. Sliding In (Like McGrain)
Big Wednesday. Energetic indie rock.

CHAMBER OF HORRORS

11 games we'd rather forget

1. Celtic 1 Inverness Caledonian Thistle 3 Scottish Cup third round, 8 February 2000
Defeat against Hearts (having been 2-0 up) three days earlier had been a sickener, but it was about to get so much worse. Master tactician John Barnes decided to supplement Mark Viduka and Mark Burchill with Lubo Moravcik and Eyal Berkovic pushing on from midfield, leaving Colin Healy and Regi Blinker to do the legwork. Or not. "I couldn't see it happening before the game," said Barnes. "But after the first half an hour you could see it." No shit, Sherlock. As if that wasn't bad enough, the dressing room is well and truly 'lost' at half-time when Viduka, whose anger had been festering for months, squared up to coach Eric Black after a suggestion that his heart wasn't in it. Viduka took his boots off and refused to play the second-half. The others, trailing 2-1, might as well not have re-emerged either. Caley grabbed a third and well, you all know the headline next morning. By the end of the day, Barnes was gone.

2. Neuchatel Xamax 5 Celtic 1 UEFA Cup, second round, first leg, 22 October 1991
The bleakest night – and the heaviest defeat in European competition – as the Swiss side with a Sassenach boss (Roy Hodgson) run riot. "I had watched them play and didn't think they were better than us in any shape or form," said Liam Brady. It's hard to concur. Brady's bunch played a previously untried 3-5-2 that allowed the Swiss – fielding three Egyptians – ample space down the flanks which they exploited to the full. Hossam Hassan got a hat-trick. Brian O'Neil scored for us, if anyone can still bear to read about it. Back to 4-4-2 for the return, but a 1-0 win is a long way short…

3. Celtic 0 Rapid Vienna 1 Cup Winners' Cup, second-round replay, 12 December 1984
The game that should never have been played ended with the ugly Austrians ruining Christmas. With Celtic through on aggregate after a 3-0 win at Parkhead (following a 3-1 defeat in Vienna), a third match at neutral Old Trafford was secured by the vicious-tackling Viennese. UEFA, having discredited Rapid's initial claim that

Rudi Weinhofer was hit by a bottle at Parkhead, then astonishingly uphold a second, different complaint. Namely, if it wasn't a bottle, it must have been a coin and Celtic were responsible for their fans' behaviour. Despite upping Rapid's fine from £5,000 to £10,000 for their contribution to events (midfielder Reinhard Kienast was suspended for four games for punching Tommy Burns on the back of the head) the second leg was declared 'irregular' and voided. On a night when cool heads are vital, the only ones around were speaking German. "You could see the venom on the fans' faces," said Tommy Burns. "It backfired on us." A farcical goal from Peter Pacult, after Celtic hit a post, put the Hoops out and left a lengthy shadow.

4. Raith Rovers 2 Celtic 2 (5-6 on penalties) League Cup final, 27 November 1994
It's hard not to feel sorry for Tommy Burns. Such a likeable man, his tenure as Celtic boss is remembered largely for the off-pitch troubles and this sorry showing – at Mordor, of all places. With Parkhead undergoing a facelift and home games being played at Hampden Park, Ibrox was the biggest alternative venue. Celtic came back from Stevie Crawford's goal to lead through Andy Walker and Charlie Nicholas – this with six minutes left – but Gordon Marshall's gaffe allowed ex-Gers man Gordon Dalziel to equalise. No more scoring in extra time, and with Raith 6-5 ahead in the shootout, Paul McStay's weak effort was easily saved by Scott Thomson and the legendary dancing in the streets of Kirkcaldy commenced.

5. Celtic 0 Internazionale 0 (4-5 on penalties) European Cup semi-final second leg, 19 April 1972
If you thought the Italians were negative in Lisbon in 1967, this was something else. Missing the injured Roberto Boninsegna, Milan killed the game at every opportunity. After two hours of tedium, it was down to the lottery of penalties to settle who would compete for the biggest prize in European football. After Evan Williams got a hand to Mazzola's kick but was unable to keep it out, it was Dixie Deans's turn. His kick sailed high and wide. Celtic were out.

6. Rangers 5 Celtic 1 7 August 1988
As wake-up calls go, this was about as rude as it gets. Just three weeks earlier Billy McNeill, who'd led us to the centenary title a few months earlier, was gladhanded as he was driven round Parkhead in a green Roller. A Mini would have been a better indication of the way things were headed. The only summer signing had been keeper Ian Andrews for £300,000. Andrews, covering here for an injured Packie Bonner and with scant protection from Mick McCarthy and Roy Aitken, lasted nine games in a Celtic shirt. He was so bad that Alan Rough was called for instead. The Hoops eventually trailed in a sorry third, ten points behind Rangers, and you know what happened during the following eight seasons.

7. Celtic 0 Aberdeen 0 (8-9 on penalties) Scottish Cup final, 12 May 1990
The first penalty shootout in a Scottish Cup final started badly when Dariuz
Wdowczyk fired wide, but things picked up when Brian Grant failed to convert
Aberdeen's fourth. It was nail-biting time as all the rest were scored, leaving Anton
Rogan to try his luck at 8-8. It wasn't in.

8. Celtic 1 Partick Thistle 4 Scottish League Cup final, 23 October 1971
With 'Caesar' McNeill absent and Jinky forced off after 20 minutes, it was all downhill.
Partick zipped into a four-goal lead inside 40 minutes and took their first silverware
for half a century. Jock Stein described it as "the biggest blow we've ever had".

9. Dunfermline Athletic 2 Celtic 0 Scottish Cup final replay, 26 April 1961
Jock Stein, a year earlier Celtic's reserve-team boss, returned to haunt the Hoops and
give the Pars a first piece of silverware with a 2-0 win. Supporters issued a collective
groan at the tinkering of chairman Robert Kelly – in charge of all first-team matters,
with Jimmy McGrory manager in name only – and prepared for more mediocrity.
Still, the Big Man would be back in four years and things could only get better…

10. Celtic 0 Atletico Madrid 0 European Cup semi-final first leg, 10 April 1974
Ah, the majesty of Spanish football – the culture of Real, the passion of Barça and
the animals of Atletico Madrid. From the off at Celtic Park the visitors ran through
the big book of Johnny Foreigner cheats, meting out special treatment to Jimmy
Johnstone. They ended up with eight men, and a 0-0 draw. The mastermind behind
this approach? Argentinian Juan Carlos Lorenzo, who'd managed his country's
notorious 1966 World Cup side. Expectations that the tie would be awarded to
the Hoops as a punishment failed to come to fruition, and Celtic headed to Madrid,
where death threats to Jinky and the Big Man were received and the team lost 2-0,
falling at the semi-final hurdle for the second time in three years.

11. Motherwell 2 Celtic 1 Scottish Premier League, Fir Park, 21 May 2005
There have been some desperate moments in our history, but this was something
else. Needing a win to take the title, Sutton's 25th-minute goal looked to have done
the job. With 120 seconds to go, the champagne corks are being eased out – in
the helicopter hovering between Fir Park and Easter Road (where Rangers are
beating Hibs 1-0) they're tieing on the green-and-white ribbons. Even Martin
O'Neill is contemplating breathing out. Then Scott McDonald – a Hoops fan from
Down Under – turns our world upside down. His scissor-kick shreds our title hopes,
his 90th-minute winner adds insult to injury. The helicopter hovering between Fir
Park and Easter Road wheels away and we're left with a handful of dust. Martin
O'Neill's swansong, if that's what it proves to be, should never have been like this.

CLASSIC NICKNAMES

Lemon to Boris, and a beautiful through ball to Rhino...

1. Baby Elephant Robert Campbell

2. Disco King Jacky Dziekanowski

3. Flying Flea or **Jinky** Jimmy Johnstone

4. Obliterator Willie Loney

5. Buzz-bomb Bobby Lennox, also known as **Lemon**. The name was given him by Willie Wallace after a misspelled newspaper report

6. Caesar Billy McNeill. After the team went to see *Ocean's XI*, he was renamed after star Cesar Romero and the spelling was bastardised

7. The Quality Street Gang a collective sobriquet (hey!) for young tyros McGrain, Macari, Connelly and Hay at the start of the 1970s

8. Wee Rhino Murdo MacLeod. Can't think why

9. Jackie **Boris** McNamara after young Jackie's dad (of the same name) who also played for Celtic and was so dubbed for his communist leanings

10. Charles de Goal, Slick Nick, Bonnie Prince Charlie, Champagne Charlie, Cannonball Kid Charlie Nicholas. Almost a team in itself!

11. Bomb Scare Olivier Tebily. Well, that was the impression given by the defence every time the ball went near it when he played…

CLEOPATRA'S NOSE MOMENTS

Events that inadvertently changed Celtic history

1. Charity begins at home…
At a dinner to celebrate Hibernian's 1887 Scottish Cup final victory over Dumbarton, Brother Walfrid of Glasgow's Marist Order, impressed with what he's seen, decides to form a football team to raise money for charitable causes. Celtic is born.

2. If you build it, they will come…

Celtic play Queen's Park in the opening round of the 1889/90 Scottish Cup. A crowd of 26,000 – the highest attendance yet for a match between two Scottish teams – makes it clear turning professional is the way forward.

3. In a league of our own

At a meeting at Holton's Hotel, Glasford Street, Glasgow, on 20 March 1890, committee member John McLaughlin suggests the formation of a Scottish League similar to the one in England. Almost exactly five months later, Celtic kick off the club's inaugural league campaign with a 4-1 defeat by Renton.

4. Parkhead life

In 1892 the club leaves its old ground (by the Eastern Necropolis) after the landlord decides to raise the rent from £50 to £450. The new Celtic Park – built partly by Irish labourers on a voluntary basis – has a 70,000 capacity. "Like leaving the graveyard to enter paradise," says one wag, and a nickname is born.

5. Public image limited

After a long struggle, amateurism finally gives way to professionalism and Celtic become a limited liability company on 4 March 1897. The lease on Celtic Park is purchased later that year for £10,000 and Willie Maley becomes secretary-manager.

6. Kicking and screaming

Belfast shipbuilders Harland and Wolff open a yard on the Clyde in 1912. An imported Irish Protestant workforce, antagonistic to Catholicism, finds an outlet in football with fervent support of Rangers, already Celtic's major rivals. The final day of the 1921/22 season, in which Celtic took the league by a point from Rangers with a draw at Morton, is marred by rioting on the terraces. The 'Old Firm' term, incidentally, had been coined eight years earlier in a cartoon in *The Scottish Referee* newspaper.

MCGRAIN, MACARI, CONNELLY AND HAY WERE BETTER KNOWN AS 'THE QUALITY STREET GANG'

7. Talk of the Crown

The 1953 Coronation Cup win. Celtic, in the doldrums since World War 2, defeat the might of Arsenal, Manchester United and Hibs in an all-Scottish final to banish the misery of years of underachievement. Pride in the jersey is visible once more. Next season's Double – the first title since 1937/38 – is especially notable given that Celtic claw back a seven-point deficit in February to overtake Hearts with a nine-game winning streak at the close of the campaign.

8. The Big Man's back

Jock Stein's arrival as boss in March 1965. Chairman Robert Kelly, having effectively run the team for two decades, finally concedes that he's not up to the job. After a protracted series of negotiations in which Stein is offered first an assistant manager's post to Sean Fallon and then a joint role, the Big Man signs on the dotted line on 10 March – with full control. An 8-0 win over Aberdeen the day before suggests the players are in tune with the news.

9. Billy Bhoy

Billy McNeill's header nine minutes from time against Dunfermline Athletic – the club Stein had transformed to make his name – in the 1965 Scottish Cup final acts as a catalyst for the most glorious era in the club's history. A snapshot of this goal occupied a prominent position on the wall of Stein's office.

10. The man McCann

After a bitter struggle for control, bespectacled Scots exile Fergus McCann (who has made his fortune in Canada) assumes control at Parkhead on Friday 4 March 1994. The businessman eventually brings an end to a century of control by the White and Kelly families, who have presided over Celtic's decline as Rangers have modernised. Celtic Park is a changed place – to the tune of £41m – for his involvement. A boycott of the game against Kilmarnock three days before McCann took over had seen just 10,882 turn up. As the curtain went up on the 1998/99 season, Celtic had 53,000 season-ticket holders and the highest average attendance in British football.

11. 'Demolition Derby'

Celtic 6 Rangers 2 (27 August 2000). Martin O'Neill's first taste of Old Firm action starts with a bang – a totally unexpected all-guns-blazing display totally out of character with the more guarded approach everyone was expecting. Full of confidence after wiping the floor with Dick Advocaat's men, the Bhoys romp to the league title with five games to spare – and beat Rangers at Ibrox for the first time in six years. Larsson ends up with 53 goals and the Golden Shoe in the process.

CLOSE, BUT NO CIGAR

11 chronic underachievers

1. Joe Carruth 1936-45

Reckoned the closest Celtic ever came to a new Jimmy Quinn or Jimmy McGrory, he drifted away after a series of loan spells but still managed 30 goals in 42 outings.

2. Stewart Kerr 1994-2001
Such a good prospect that we sold Shay Given to Newcastle. With Bonner imperious, Kerr didn't get a chance to impress until Tommy Burns arrived – and fluffed his lines against Falkirk. Taxi for Kerr to Wigan!

3. Dariuz 'Jacki' Dziekanowski 1989-92
The nicknames 'Disco King', 'the George Best of Poland', and 'Playboy of the Eastern World' suggest his mind wasn't always 100 per cent on his football. Roy Aitken described him as a natural entertainer and he was likened to Charlie Nicholas, but his form was up and down – great or, frankly, shite. Liam Brady shipped him out to Bristol City in January 1992. By August he was on about moving again…

4. Gerry Creaney 1987-94
Hailed as one of the brightest prospects for years, he bagged 23 goals alongside Tommy Coyne and Charlie Nicholas in 1991/92. Injuries hampered his progress and he was not fancied by Liam Brady or Lou Macari. Joined Portsmouth for £600,000 where he enjoyed moderate success in a struggling team.

5. Paul Byrne 1993-95
He was Northern Ireland Player – and Young Player – of the Year when he was snapped up for £70,000 in May 1993. He made his full debut in Brady's last stand but the fag-end of the Brady era was a tough time to be 21. He had a neat touch and could hit a fine cross too, but had left for Southend United by 1995.

6. Steve Fulton 1987-93
Billy McNeill flew the flag for this Celtic Boys' Club graduate as an outstanding prospect. A great game against Hibs in the semi of the 1989 Scottish Cup was the highlight for this midfielder from Greenock. Six seasons down the line from his debut he was off to Bolton Wanderers, where he spent much of his time in the stiffs. Looked like he enjoyed a pie, too.

7. Danny Crainie 1979-83
One of Sean Fallon's last acquisitions, Puffer got a goal just 90 seconds into his Old Firm debut on 10 April 1982 and a hat-trick a fortnight later against Partick Thistle. But that was as good as it got and Davie Hay shipped him out to Wolverhampton Wanderers within a year.

8. Vic Davidson 1968-75
Made a promising start after converting from midfielder to striker, but ebbed away after a poor showing in a defeat by Rangers in September 1974. "Demoralised" by

reserve-team football, he joined Motherwell. He returned to Celtic under Billy McNeill in March 1979, but again failed to impress.

9. Robert Hannah 1974-77
Named as one of three to watch in April 1975 by no less than Jock Stein, Hannah had been part of the Bhoys' U17 European Youth Cup-winning side a year earlier. Despite being part of the squads for Euro away trips to Sachsenring and Wisla Krakow in 1976, he played just three times in all.

10. Leslie Johnston 1948/49
When Celtic signed this centre-forward from Clyde in October 1948 after a six-year chase, he became the first Scot to have racked up £30,000 in combined transfer fees. After Celtic's disappointing exit to Dundee United in the Scottish Cup in January 1949, he faded fast and was sold to Stoke City in October that year.

11. Colin Healy 1998-2003
Good enough to play for his country, but not good enough to play for Celtic. Four years of attempting to get established saw him, er, fail to establish himself. Lost his way under John Barnes (join the queue, Colin) but looked like making a recovery during Martin O'Neill's early days – only to be eventually sent to Coventry.

Manager: David Hay Nine points clear of Rangers in 1986/87 but failed to win the title and paid for it with his job. A great shame given the last-gasp heroics against St Mirren that won the league in the previous year.

COLLECTABLE PROGRAMMES AND PRICES
Programmes! Programmes! Exact money please!

1. Dinamo Batumi v Celtic (European Cup Winner's Cup, 1995/96) £1,200-£1,500
Very few made the trip, so very few exist. Beware of imitations!
2. Olympiakos v Celtic (European Cup, 2 October 1974) £1,500
3. Slovan Bratislava v Celtic (European Cup Winners' Cup, 4 March 1964) £1,500
4. Aarhus v Celtic (European Cup Winners' Cup, 3 November 1965) £1,500
5. FC Zurich v Celtic (European Cup, 5 October 1967) £1,250
6. Vojvodina v Celtic (European Cup, 1 March 1967) £1,250
7. Kokkola v Celtic (European Cup, 30 September 1970) £1,000
8. Celtic v Internazionale (European Cup final, 25 May 1967) £220-£250
9. Celtic v Rangers (Scottish League Cup final, 19 October 1957) £130-£180

10. **Celtic v Motherwell** (Scottish Cup final, 21 April 1951) £125
11. **Celtic v Arsenal/Hibernian v Tottenham Hotspur** (split programme, Coronation Cup semi-final, 11 May 1953) £125
   Celtic v Manchester United/Newcastle United v Hibernian (split programme, Coronation Cup semi-final, 16 May 1953) £125
   Celtic v Hibernian (Coronation Cup final, 20 May 1953) £125

COME TO SEE CELTIC?

11 humungous Hoops gates

1. **146,433** v Aberdeen, Scottish Cup final, 24 April 1937. *Still the record gate for a European club match.*
2. **136,505** v Leeds United, European Cup semi-final second leg, Hampden Park, 15 April 1970. *The largest crowd for a match in European club competition.*
3. **132,842** v Hearts, Scottish Cup final, 21 April 1956
4. **131,943** v Motherwell, Scottish Cup final, 21 April 1951
5. **129,926** v Aberdeen, Scottish Cup final, 24 April 1954
6. **129,527** v Rangers, Scottish Cup final, 4 May 1963
7. **126,599** v Rangers, Scottish Cup final, 23 April 1966
8. **126,102** v Aberdeen, Scottish Cup final, 29 April 1967
9. **120,263** v Rangers, Scottish Cup final replay, 15 May 1963
10. **120,000** v Racing Club, World Club Championship, 18 October 1967
11. **118,730** v Rangers, League Division One, 2 January 1939

CULT HEROES

We are not worthy...

1. Jock Stein

One European Cup, ten league titles, eight Scottish Cups and six League Cups in 13 years. His playing role in pulling Celtic out of the doldrums after the war is an understated part of his story – he was as good as player-manager when he captained the Double-winners of 1953/54 – and his part in the club's greatest stories can never be overstated.

COLIN HEALY LOST HIS WAY UNDER JOHN BARNES (JOIN THE QUEUE, COLIN)

2. Jimmy Johnstone

Irrepressible, on and off the pitch. Whether joking with opponents twice his size about swapping shirts before the biggest game in the club's history (the 1967 European Cup final), having to be rescued by coastguards while adrift in a rowing boat, or taking endless calls from Jock Stein in Glasgow pubs telling him to go home, the man was a one-off. It's galling to see such an athlete stricken with motor neurone disease.

3. Jimmy McGrory

British football's most prolific scorer – and hardly likely to be beaten any time soon. He managed the Bhoys for close on 20 years after World War 2. After refusing to leave for Arsenal in 1928, his loyalty to the Hoops scandalously cost him a wage reduction for the rest of his Parkhead career. Vies with Jock Stein for the title of Mr Celtic.

4. Lubo Moravcik

"A gift from God" in the words of Celtic fanzine *Not The View*. Spot on – and a far cry from the hacks' reaction when Jo Venglos paid Duisberg tuppence for this Slovakian 33-year-old in November 1998. A cracking debut in a 6-1 hammering of Dundee showed us just what he could do. He followed that with another masterclass in the 5-1 mauling of Rangers. He was once asked, through an interpreter, what it was like to go from a zero to a hero. "Tell him I was never a zero," was his flat reply. Ask Martin O'Neill who was at the heart of the Treble-winning side. He'll soon tell you.

5. Henrik Larsson

TULLEY SCORED DIRECT FROM A CORNER. ORDERED TO RETAKE IT, HE REPEATED THE FEAT

Some thought it clever to boo him when we met Barcelona, but then some people have very short memories. To be as good as he was after his leg-break against Lyon tells you all you need to know about the man. Have you ever seen a photo of his feet? How do you think they came to look like that? From giving everything, game in, game out, that's how. Fit to grace any Celtic era.

6. Charlie Tulley

Off-the-pitch antics annoyed his team-mates and the club's management, but he was the terrace darling between 1948 and 1959. Scored directly from a corner against Falkirk in 1954. When ordered to take it again, he repeated the feat.

7. Dixie Deans

Dig those naff forward-roll goal celebrations! Who needs somersaults? Spitting out blood through the gap recently occupied by his front teeth against St Johnstone in January 1976, he carried on regardless. That's the definition of 'jersey player' for you. Just 5ft 8in tall, but possessed of boundless energy and a phenomenal appetite for goals. A childhood Rangers fan, but you'd never have known.

8. Davie Provan

Billy McNeill's first signing – a Scottish record buy at £120,000 from Kilmarnock in March 1978 – was a diehard Rangers fan who embraced the cause. So much so in fact, that the winger once taunted Rangers' Alex McDonald with: "I could keep a beach ball off you in a telephone booth." Four titles, two Scottish Cups and a Scottish League Cup followed. His trademark socks-round-the-ankles look and curly perm made him stand out – as did one of his free-kick specials which levelled the 1985 Scottish Cup final against Dundee United. ME – from which he thankfully recovered – brought his career to a premature end in 1987.

9. Murdo MacLeod

"Big-bummed and barrel-chested", the Wee Rhino was a local lad who arrived from Dumbarton for £100,000 in 1978. Another 100-per-center, he was the midfield heartbeat for the next nine seasons – winning three league titles, two Scottish Cups and a League Cup. He also had the happy knack of bagging vital Old Firm goals – the clincher in 1979's 4-2 win, the 25-yarder in the 4-4 draw in March 1986 and the winner in the 1983 League Cup final.

10. Charlie Nicholas

Can you imagine him as a sweeper? That's the position from which he was converted to striker with the Celtic Boys Club U16s. Smart move – Jock Stein signed him shortly afterwards. A true cavalier, the Champagne Charlie tag was highly apt. A goal on his home debut against Clyde early in 1979/80 set the tone – 46 more in 1982/83 gave him the pick of Arsenal, Liverpool or Manchester United. Should he have stayed put? Perhaps. He'd have won more medals. But he did eventually come home – and his sublime goal against Rangers in the 2-0 Easter win at Ibrox in 1992 was a rare reminder of quality in those long, lean years.

11. Peter Grant

If you wanted sweat, here's your man. Missing from the team that clinched the 1987/88 title at Dundee (having broken his foot against St Mirren), his name was chanted until he came out – on his crutches. A real battler who overcame a hepatitis scare, he made his first visit to Ibrox on his debut in 1984 – that's how much he loved the club. His dislike for Rangers was never more evident than in the 1991 Scottish Cup final, where he joined Walters, Hurlock and Hateley in an early dismissal.

D'OH! 11 GREAT ERRORS OF JUDGEMENT

If I could have my life all over again...

1. Buys from Brazil
John Barnes splashes out £5m on Brazilian Scheidt late in 1999. He might as well have stuck a sign saying 'Do not employ me in football again' on his forehead.

2. Ministry of defence
All the defending during the 8-0 defeat by Motherwell on 30 April 1937 – it remains the club's heaviest loss in any competition.

3. Billy don't be a hero
Billy McNeill leaves Celtic Park in the summer of 1983 for Manchester City after a rift with the board. He refuses to apologise for statements made in the press – that he denied making – concerning his salary, and also refuses to replace right-hand man John Clark with Frank Connor. After finding a ready-made replacement for Stein, Celtic send themselves back to square one.

4. The Brady crunch
Having blown £1.1m on Tony Cascarino in the summer of 1991, Liam Brady realises he's out of his depth as boss at Parkhead – probably pretty soon after watching Cas in the Hoops. The 5-1 UEFA Cup thrashing by Neuchatel Xamax crystallises everybody's worst fears by November.

5. Skip to the Lou
Lou Macari returns to Celtic as boss in 1993/94, against the advice of friends. A promising start becomes a swimming-against-the-tide affair as lack of funds forces him to bring in jobbing Englishmen. The nadir? The 4-2 defeat at the Death Star on New Year's Day 1994, when missiles were lobbed at the directors' box. The boycott of

a game against Kilmarnock in March resulted in a crowd of just 10,402. Emerging from the internecine strife, new MD Fergus McCann hands Macari his P45. Macari took the club to court for £400,000 but eventually lost his case in 1997.

6. Money to Burns
A hero of six league championships, Tommy Burns's tenure in the Parkhead hot seat is remembered fondly, but mainly by supporters of Raith Rovers. If Raith's penalty shootout victory in the 1994 Scottish League Cup final wasn't bad enough, 11 games without a win that year in exile at Hampden Park saw Burns claim an unwanted club record. A dour 1995 Scottish Cup final win over Airdrie was as good as it got – and one sole defeat in 1995/96 still only bought second place behind Rangers. Burns's three-year contract – marked in its latter stages by childish squabbling among foreign stars Pierre van Hooijdonk, Jorge Cadete and Paolo Di Canio – was not renewed in 1997.

7. Handbag sale
After the 1909 Scottish Cup final finishes with no extra time in sight, 'The Hampden Riot' ensues as fans protest at the lack of a winner. Fuelled by the notion that this is to force a lucrative replay, the mob turns angry, using goalposts to attack police. The SFA withheld the trophy and Celtic and Rangers were forced to pay £150 each for repairs. You try and tell young people today that, and they won't believe you.

8. Right-back where we started
Chairman John Kelly – a regular tinkerer with the team during Jimmy McGrory's post-war years – inexplicably chooses to field greenhorn Billy Craig, just 20, at right-back against Hearts in the 1956 Scottish Cup final, while regular right-back Mike Haughney plays at inside-right. The result was a 3-1 defeat.

9. To lose five managers is unfortunate...
The old 'if it ain't broke, don't fix it' mantra is cheerfully ignored as Celtic appoint Jock Brown as general manager in the summer of 1997. Wim Jansen, about to do the Hoops rather nicely as gaffer, crosses swords with Brown. Ultimately, a stylish 48 hours after winning the league – and more importantly preventing Ranger's tenth consecutive title – he turns his office lights off for the last time. Celtic begin the search for a new manager for the sixth time in a decade.

10. It's the way you pick 'em
Spring 1999 and new chief executive Allan McDonald offers golfing buddy Kenny Dalglish the post of director of football at Celtic. "Great," says Kenny. "John Barnes will make an excellent coach." Don't pick my lottery numbers, mate.

11. Luck of the draw
Gordon Marshall spoons the ball to Raith's Gordon Dalziel for an equaliser at the death in the aforementioned League Cup final – our first final for four years. And it's at Ibrox.

DON'T FORGET TO WRITE…

Old bhoys who came back to haunt us

1. Mo Johnston
The great defector. Not only did he join Rangers, he added insult to injury by scoring in an Old Firm clash. "For a while I did unite Rangers and Celtic fans," he joked. "There were people in both camps that hated me." Very funny.

2. Charlie Nicholas
Ouch! Scored in the penalty shootout for Aberdeen in the 1990 Scottish Cup final. A dark, dark day, especially if your name is Anton Rogan.

3. Mark Burchill
The nearly man who took a tilt at the title charge in April's 2-0 win for Hearts at Parkhead. Cheers!

4. Bryan Prunty
The former Celtic trainee enjoys the immutable law of the former player when he equalises as a substitute for Aberdeen at Parkhead in April 2004. The Dons go on to steal it at the death.

5. Tommy Gemmell
The Lisbon Lion is jeered by the boo-boys after Dundee beat the Bhoys 1-0 in the 1973 Scottish League Cup final. There's gratitude for you.

6. Harald Brattbakk
Mostly rubbish with the Hoops, but looked better for Rosenborg. Especially when he scored both goals in a 2-0 win in the 2001/02 Champions League over Celtic.

7. Henrik Larsson
Just looked plain wrong in a Barcelona kit. Even more wrong when scoring the third goal in it against us at the Nou Camp in 2003/04.

8. Kenny Dalglish
Returned for Jock Stein's testimonial with Liverpool in August 1978, having left Parkhead a year earlier. Liverpool won 3-2 and Dalglish was given a cool reception, to say the least.

9. Tommy Coyne
Der Bomber bombs us out of the Scottish Cup at the third-round stage in January 1994 for Motherwell at Fir Park.

10. Mike Conroy
Embarrassed the Hoops by masterminding a 2-0 friendly success as player-manager of Cork City in August 1991. One of Liam Brady's first games.

11. Kenny Dalglish
Yes, he's already appeared once in this list. But playing in a testimonial is one thing, recommending John Barnes for the top job is a different crime altogether.

DOPPELGANGERS

11 players with double identities

1. **Andy Bell** early Celtic keeper helps out with vocal duties for Erasure
2. **Michael Jackson** no jokes about young Bhoys, please
3. **James Oliver** no informal 'Jamie' for Celtic keeper turned TV chef
4. **John Kennedy** safe hands between the sticks for the President of the US
5. **John Thomson** tragic goalkeeper comes back as *Fast Show* comic
6. **Tommy Boyd** centre-half and *Magpie* presenter
7. **James Cameron** handy to offer direction in a Titanic struggle
8. **Chris Morris** right-back turned TV satirist
9. **John Hughes** striker morphs into US teen flick merchant
10. **John Joseph O'Neill** jockeying for position?
11. **John Smith** political footballer

Subs: John McNamara and **John McNamee**
Legendary Aussie tennis doubles pairing change first names to complete spurious list

> HENRIK LARSSON JUST LOOKED PLAIN WRONG IN A BARCELONA SHIRT

EARLY DOORS

11 straight knock-outs in Europe

1. Valencia 6-4 on aggregate in the 1962/63 Inter-Cities Fairs Cup
2. Dynamo Kiev 3-2 on aggregate in the 1967/68 European Cup
3. Olympiakos 3-1 on aggregate in the 1974/75 European Cup
4. Wisla Krakow 4-2 on aggregate in the 1976/77 UEFA Cup
5. Politechnica Timisoara 2-2 on aggregate in the 1980/81 European Cup Winners' Cup. Lost on away goals
6. Juventus 2-1 on aggregate in the 1981/82 European Cup
7. Atletico Madrid 3-2 on aggregate in the 1985/86 European Cup Winners' Cup
8. Borussia Dortmund 3-2 on aggregate in the 1987/88 UEFA Cup
9. Partizan Belgrade 6-6 on aggregate in the 1989/90 European Cup Winners' Cup. Lost on away goals
10. Hamburg 4-0 on aggregate in the 1996/97 UEFA Cup
11. Croatia Zagreb 3-1 on aggregate in the 1998/99 Champions League, second qualifying round

EBAY TRINKETS

11 Celtic-related bits of tat

1. Retro sew-on patch badge £1.99
2. 'John Hartson is God' badge £0.99
3. 2oz tobacco tin £1.99
4. The Celtic Huddle painting £5
5. Three-piece towel set £8.99
6. Aiden McGeady limited-edition print £23
7. Subbuteo team £10
8. The Simpsons as Celtic fans, drinking coaster £2.25
9. Enamelled cufflinks £6.18

11 EUROPEAN CUP FINAL 1970

Evan Williams

David Hay — Tommy Gemmell

Bobby Murdoch — Billy McNeill — Jim Brogan

Jimmy Johnstone — Bobby Lennox
Willie Wallace — Bertie Auld
John Hughes

The Celtic side that reached the European Cup final on 6 May 1970, only to lose 2-1 in extra time to Feyenoord at the San Siro.

10. **Lossiemouth 1992 friendly programme** 99p
11. **Bobby Petta autograph (genuine)** £1.99. How much for a forged one?

ENGLAND, THEIR ENGLAND

11 players who flew south

1. **Charlie Nicholas** Arsenal
2. **Frank McAvennie** West Ham United
3. **Mark Viduka** Leeds United
4. **Willie Wallace** Crystal Palace
5. **Bertie Auld** Birmingham City
6. **Bobby Murdoch** Middlesbrough
7. **Craig Burley** Derby County
8. **George McCluskey** Leeds United
9. **Simon Donnelly** Sheffield Wednesday
10. **Phil O'Donnell** Sheffield Wednesday
11. **Dixie Deans** Luton Town
Sub: **Mark Burchill** Portsmouth

11. EUROPEAN CUP WINNERS 1967

Ronnie Simpson

Jim Craig   Tommy Gemmell

Bobby Murdoch   Billy McNeill   John Clark

Jimmy Johnstone   Bobby Lennox
Willie Wallace   Bertie Auld
Steve Chalmers

The first British team to lift the European Cup, beating Internazionale 2-1 at the National Stadium, Lisbon on 25 May 1967.

EURO VISIONS

11 memorable nights in European competitions

1. Celtic 2 Internazionale 1 European Cup final, National Stadium, Lisbon, 25 May 1967
If you don't know this by now, you haven't paid attention. Go back and start again.

2. Celtic 2 Porto 3 UEFA Cup final, Stadio Olimpico, Seville, 21 May 2003
Okay, so we lost to the cheating Portuguese-Brazilian dwarf, his histrionic mates and their 'special' manager. But 80,000 fans mobbing Seville – who could forget that? Now, what happened in that episode of *The Bill* again?

3. Celtic 2 Leeds United 1 European Cup semi-final second leg, Hampden Park, 15 April 1970
A record crowd for a European fixture – 136,505 – squeezes into Hampden. Billy Bremner's long-range effort cancels out the Hoops's 1-0 advantage from the first leg, but two goals in five minutes just after half-time from John Hughes and Bobby Murdoch settle the 'Battle of Britain' to set up a showdown with Feyenoord in Milan. In 1965 Don Revie had claimed Scottish football would be dead by 1970. Aye, right.

4. Celtic 2 Vojvodina Novi Sad 0 European Cup quarter-final, second leg, Parkhead, 8 March 1967
In front of a tense, but ultimately delirious 75,000 crowd, Billy McNeill's last-minute header from Charlie Gallagher's corner doubles the lead achieved through Stevie Chalmers' 60th-minute goal to send the Bhoys through 2-1 on aggregate. Tommy Gemmell recalled the tie as "our hardest two matches in all my years in Europe".

5. Celtic 3 Dukla Prague 1 European Cup semi-final, first leg, Parkhead, 12 April 1967
Two-goal Willie Wallace, signed from Hearts four months earlier, is the hero when the visitors' slick movement and passing are a joy to watch. Strunc had cancelled out an opening goal from Jimmy Johnstone, nipping in to beat keeper Jan Viktor.

6. Celtic 2 Real Madrid 0 European Cup quarter-final first leg, 19 March 1980
The official crowd is 67,000 but estimates are nearer 80-90,000 as the Hoops's young hopefuls, Murdo MacLeod and Davie Provan – and Bobby Lennox – see off the Spanish giants with goals from George McCluskey and Johnny Doyle.

7. Celtic 6 SC Tirol Innsbruck 3 UEFA Cup, second qualifying round, second leg, Parkhead, 26 August 1997
For high-octane excitement, it doesn't get any better. A 7-5 aggregate victory for the Celts – eventually – in front of a 47,000 crowd. More swings than a PGA golf tournament as a Larsson own-goal brings the Austrians back to 2-2 at half-time; Celtic forge ahead for 4-2, concede again to level the aggregate at 5-5, but putting Innsbruck ahead on away goals. Then Morten Wieghorst and Craig Burley put Celtic through on an unforgettable night in which the lead changed hands seven times.

8. Celtic 4 Juventus 3 Champions League, Group E, Parkhead, 31 October 2001
Win or bust – or win and bust. This encounter with the Old Lady was one of the best European contests for years. Lubo Moravcik pulls the strings as the Hoops come from a goal down to win with strikes from Joos Valgaeren, Chris Sutton twice, and a Larsson penalty. Porto's 1-0 win over Rosenborg means an exit from the UEFA Cup, but what a game…

9. Celtic 5 Red Star Belgrade 1 European Cup second-round, first leg, Parkhead, 13 November 1968
With the score 1-1 at half-time, Jock Stein promises Jimmy Johnstone – terrified of flying since an incident holidaying in America two years earlier – that he won't have to travel to Belgrade if he turns it on after the break. Et voila! The inspirational Jinky scores twice and sets up two more for Bobby Lennox and Willie Wallace.

10. Ajax 1 Celtic 2 European Cup first round, second leg, Amsterdam ArenA,
29 Sept 1982
Having drawn the first leg 2-2, there are few bets backing the Hoops. Johan Cruyff
et al are beaten on their own patch with a backs-to-the-wall display in which Packie
Bonner excels, Charlie Nicholas scores a pearler, and sub George McCluskey does
a Stevie Chalmers, deflecting Danny McGrain's shot in for the winner.

11. Liverpool 0 Celtic 2 UEFA Cup quarter-final, second leg, Anfield, April 2003
John Hartson's brilliant second goal secures a semi-final spot and a 3-1 aggregate
win on a night of classic counter-attacking. Anfield justice at last for 1965/66.

EVER-PRESENTS

Great and good dependables and the league campaigns they served in

1. **Pat Bonner** 1980/81, 1981/82, 1982/83, 1989/90, 1990/91
2. **Tommy Gemmell** 1965/66, 1966/67, 1967/68
   Billy McNeill 1967/68, 1968/69, 1971/72
4. **Bobby Evans** 1952/53, 1954/55
   John Clark 1965/66, 1966/67
   Michael Haughney 1954/55, 1956/57
   Bertie Peacock 1950/51, 1953/54
   Roy Aitken 1978/79, 1985/86
   Paul McStay 1982/83, 1987/88
   Murdo MacLeod 1979/80, 1981/82
11. **Charlie Tulley** 1948/49
    Joe Baillie, Bobby Collins, Sean Fallon 1951/52
    John Divers 1961/62
    Stevie Chalmers, John Fallon 1963/64
    Bobby Murdoch 1967/68
    Danny McGrain, Pat Stanton 1976/77
    Roddie McDonald 1977/78
    Peter Latchford 1979/80
    Mark Reid 1981/82
    Chris Morris 1987/88
    Gordon Marshall 1995/96

FIRSTS

Call me number one

1. First goal
Neil McCallum, against Rangers appropriately enough, in a 5-2 friendly victory on 28 May 1888. The teams share a convivial drink – how times change.

2. First match played at Celtic Park
The first match played at Celtic Park on 8 May 1888 was an unusual affair, with Edinburgh's Hibernian taking on Cowlairs. Hibernian were the inspiration behind the founding of Celtic and seemed the obvious choice to play the first game at the new stadium in the absence of a formalised Celtic squad.

3 First Scottish Cup final
Took place on 9 February 1889. Disappointment in a 2-1 defeat by Third Lanark.

4. First Scottish Cup
The date, 9 April 1892. An emphatic 5-1 replay victory over Queen's Park at Ibrox Park, after the first encounter is played out as a friendly following pitch invasions.

5. First league title
In 1892/93 Celtic took the title by a point from Rangers, clinching it with a 3-1 win over Leith in the penultimate game of the season on 9 May.

6. First Scottish League and Cup Double
Hearts are seen off 3-0 at Hampden Park and on 20 April 1907, history is made.

7. First League Cup win
A resounding 3-0 win over Partick Thistle on 31 October 1956, with goals from John McPhail (2) and Bobby Collins, is tempered by the fact that the players don't receive their medals until the following January. No, we don't understand it either.

11. FIRST SCOTTISH LEAGUE GAME

Jamie Bell

Jerry Reynolds   Mick McKeown

Willie Maley   Jimmy Kelly   James McLaren

John Madden   Barney Crossan
    Peter Dowds   Mick Dunbar
            Willie Groves

The historic line-up for Celtic's first Scottish league game on 23 August 1890. Celtic beat Hearts 5-0 at Tynecastle. Renton had been Celtic's first league opponents on 16 August 1890, but the Bhoys's 4-1 reverse was expunged from the records and Renton were expelled from the league.

8. First European tie
Inter-Cities Fairs Cup, 26 September and 24 October 1963. Valencia put Celtic out 6-4 over two legs.

9. First Proddy manager
Jock Stein, who took the reins in 1965.

10. First game on a Sunday
Celtic take a liking to the Sabbath with a 6-1 Scottish Cup third-round win over Clydebank, 27 January 1974. Dixie Deans scores three.

11. First Celtic manager never to have played for the club
Liam Brady. The Irishman bowled up for the 1991/92 season.

FLIES IN THE OINTMENT

11 teams who've been a thorn in our side

1. Rangers
Well, they're not likely to go away after 118 years, are they?

2. Inverness Caledonian Thistle
The dismal Scottish Cup exit on 8 February 2000 spells the end for John Barnes. Thanks for, er, nothing.

3. Raith Rovers
The 1994/95 League Cup final. Dancing in Kirckaldy, maybe, but it's a wake for the green-and-white half of Glasgow.

4. Dundee United
The only team to beat Jock Stein's 1966/67 Lisbon Lions all season. And they managed it twice.

5. Aberdeen
Fergie's 1983/84 title-winners won two and drew another of four league meetings as we finished runners-up.

6. Dunfermline Athletic
1967/68 Scottish Cup first round. The club that Stein built came back to haunt him, exacting partial revenge on the holders for defeat in the final three seasons earlier. Almost spoiled the Larsson farewell party in 2004, too…

7. Atletico Madrid
Jock Stein called them animals. A visit to the jungle saw them behave accordingly – three men off in the drawn European Cup semi-final first leg of 1973/74. They also did for the Hoops again in the European Cup Winners' Cup of 1985/86.

8. Rapid Vienna
Celtic shouldn't have had to play them again. We'd already beaten them fair and square in the 1984/85 Cup Winners' Cup. A second farcical appeal for the 'coin throwing' incident was upheld and we lost our cool in a bitter atmosphere at neutral Old Trafford. We may have the same kit but we've nothing else in common.

9. Hearts
Not content dumping Celtic out of the Scottish Cup in the fourth round, the Jambos

took seven points from us in 1986/87 – points that would have allowed the Hoops to overhaul Rangers.

10. Falkirk
The end is nigh for Tommy Burns after the Bairns knock Celtic out of the Scottish Cup semis in 1996/97. They also did for us at the fourth-round stage in 1992/93.

11. Motherwell
Trips to Fir Park will never be the same again after 21 May 2005. The only thing worse than losing the title with two minutes to go, is losing the title with two minutes to go to a side managed by a former Rangers player. Ghastly.

FLOPS
11 skeletons in the Parkhead closet

1. Rafael Scheidt
Was a surname ever more appropriate? The Brazilian defender arrived for £5m on 15 December 1999 – a signing John Barnes had seen (this is true, folks) only in the wee small hours on ESPN football. "I always thought he had a funny name, but he was a Brazilian international – and getting a Brazilian international for £5m was something I didn't see as a risk," Barnes explained in Graham McColl's *The Head Bhoys*. "I much prefer watching videos. It's not necessary to go and see a player." Hmmm. Anyway, to cut a long story short, Scheidt was injured on his debut, then sidelined after having his appendix out. He played ten games all told. Clearly no risk in spending £5m there, then. And he was total rubbish. "I like footballers who are not like you," said his incredulous new boss Martin O'Neill. "I like footballers who play well."

2. Stuart Slater
Liam Brady obviously saw something in Slater during his time at West Ham – an honour most of us never had. This is the same Liam Brady who thought Neuchatel Xamax were rubbish when he watched them shortly before they beat Celtic 5-1. Slater arrived for £1.5m – that was a lot of money in August 1992.

3. Martin Hayes
You could probably have bought the entire playing staff of Hayes Town for less than the £650,000 handed to Arsenal in May 1990. The chances are that any one of them would have been a better buy too. "I didn't get the chance to be a flop," sighed

11. FIRST CELTIC V RANGERS

Michael Dolan
Eddie Pearson
James McLaughlin
Willie Maley
Jimmy Kelly
Phil Murray
Neil McCallum
Tom Maley
John Madden
Mick Dunbar
Harry Gorevin

A 5-2 winning start for Celtic in the first-ever game against rivals Rangers. The friendly was played at Celtic Park on 28 May 1888.

Hayes when he was released on a free transfer in 1993, after making just ten appearances in close on three years.

4. Tony Cascarino
A £1.1m record signing from Aston Villa in 1991. It bought us four goals in 30 games. A swap with Tom Boyd got rid of him. Wonder who got the best deal there? "Celtic played too much football to suit my game," he said. At least he's honest.

5. Pierce O'Leary
David's brother. There the similarity ends. Came from Vancouver Whitecaps but should have stayed there.

6. Anton Rogan
Not one but two penalties for handballs against Rangers in a six-week spell in 1989/90 were just a couple of his more notable gaffes. Why on earth he thought asking for a pay rise after the 1990 Scottish Cup final defeat by Aberdeen – where he missed the crucial penalty – would work is anyone's guess. Axed from the subsequent pre-season tour, he refused to train and had his wages stopped. Left for Sunderland in October 1991.

7. Juninho

Celtic's first World Cup winner he may have been, but this Bhoy from Brazil started just 14 games in seven months in 2004/05, being unable to get past Aiden McGeady for a regular start.

8. Alfie Conn

Great on his day, but that day didn't come around nearly often enough. Dodgy knees meant the purchase intended to be the natural successor to Dalglish never got the chance to fulfil the role. He left on a free transfer in April 1979 after only 37 league outings and ten goals in just over two years.

9. Olivier Tebily

Do the nicknames 'heart attack', 'bomb scare' and 'hospital pass' suggest a pattern emerging for the Ivory Coast centre-half?

10. Regi Blinker

The dreadlocked Dutch winger arrived in a swap deal for Paolo Di Canio. So how does this swapping work, exactly?

11. Henri Camara

Yes, we know he looks pretty good at Southampton. But then so does Nigel Quashie. It's an impossible job to fill Larsson's boots, sure, but he wasn't even fit to lace them when he came on loan from Wolves.

FLOUNCERS

11 tired and emotional types

1. Mo Johnston

Had the talent – 71 goals in 127 games between 1984-87 backs that up. And a mouth to match. "Johnston told me the last time we talked he wanted to stay with Celtic. Since then we have tried to contact him all over Europe, but it seems the last to know his decision is his own club." An exasperated Billy McNeill, speaking in July 1987 on the day Johnston – who had threatened to join Manchester United a year earlier – finally left for Nantes. Wonder what happened to him after that?

2. George Connelly

So much promise, so many problems. Reckoned by some to be the best Celtic discovery since the war – Jock Stein sent him out before the Cup Winners' Cup clash with Dynamo Kiev in 1966 to entertain the crowd with his ball skills. The Scottish Football Writers' Player of the Year in 1973, he walked out on the national squad in June that year over concern for his pregnant wife, and absconded from training a few months later. Unable (he said) to cope with the pressure, he left Parkhead on 27 September 1975 and went downhill fast from there. Jock Stein once said of him: "I'm more often in George Connelly's house than I am in my own mother's."

3. Jorge Cadete
Talented striker who rocked the boat over wage demands in July 1997, contributing to boss Tommy Burns's downfall. Refused to return from his native Portugal because he was unwell and feeling undervalued – make that underpaid.

> JOCK STEIN SAID OF GEORGE CONNELLY: "I'M MORE OFTEN IN HIS HOUSE THAN I AM IN MY OWN MOTHER'S"

4. Mark Viduka
Refused to go back on after half-time during the Scottish Cup debacle against Inverness Caley Thistle at Celtic Park. Yes it was terrible, but it was no worse to be watching from the stands, surely?

5. Paolo Di Canio
A cameo from Di Canio, never slow to vent his feelings, made him Celtic's tenth sending off in the game with Hearts in November 1996. The unrest and distraction caused by his mithering helped Rangers to their ninth title in a row. Grrr. Joined Sheffield Wednesday in summer 1997, having failed to return to Celtic because he was 'ill'. The more mean-spirited might have hoped it was nothing too trivial.

6. Pierre van Hooijdonk
A monstrous ego is a less attractive aspect of the talented Dutchman's make-up. He took his handbag to Nottingham Forest in 1997, where he went one better by refusing to celebrate with his team-mates and then going on strike. Still, we made a tidy £3m profit…

7. Lou Macari
We, the jury, put it to you, the pint-sized teetotaller, that on 6 January 1973, you said: "Scottish football is dying – I must better myself." Not the wisest choice of words, even less so considering Jock Stein had just had a heart attack. The £200,000 sale to Manchester United – who stepped in at the 11th hour when it looked as if he was going to Liverpool – was a record fee for a Scot and a 1970s watershed. He was fined by new boss Tommy Docherty for refusing to play in a benefit match.

8. Wim Jansen

Celtic go Dutch, said the lazier headline writers. The Dutchman went himself just 48 hours after winning the title in 1997/98, following a breakdown in relations with general manager Jock Brown in which each man blamed the other.

9. Juninho

"I want regular games," he said. And we wanted the player Middlesbrough enjoyed.

10. Mike Galloway

Had a spat with Lou Macari before the match with Raith Rovers in November 1993. He'd allegedly missed several training sessions and had been regularly fined for breaches of club discipline.

11. Jimmy Bone

A dispute at training with Jock Stein – Bone had been angling for a move and was complaining at the lack of interest – led to a transfer to Arbroath that afternoon.

FOREIGN LEGION OF HONOUR

11 Celtic greats from other lands

1. Pat Bonner Republic of Ireland

Packie's indisputably no.1.

2. Dariusz Wdowcyzk Poland

The best striker of a dead ball since Tommy Gemmell? Took a mean corner too. Arrived shortly after Jacki Dziekanowski, but these two were Poles apart.

3. Joos Valgaeren Belgium

And you thought chocolates were the tastiest Belgian export.

4. Gianbobo Balde Guinea

"Bobo's gonnae get ye…" Can't say fairer than that. A man mountain. Shame about the sending off in the 2003 UEFA Cup final, though.

5. Johan Mjallby Sweden

Henrik Larsson, Abba, Ingmar Bergman… you really are spoiling us. A better bargain than anything you'd find in IKEA, and harder.

6. Paolo Di Canio Italy
Predictably enough, it all ended in tears, but a breathtaking talent all the same.

7. Stilian Petrov Bulgaria
A slow start after a big-money move, but 'Stan the man' has become a creative hub, with an eye for the spectacular strike.

8. Lubo Moravcik Slovakia
Pavel Nedved's boyhood hero, no less. The best 33-year-old signing in the world.

9. Henrik Larsson Sweden
Imagine Henke and McGrory in the same line-up…

10. Chris Sutton England
Worth his weight in gold up front or at the back.

11. Andreas Thom Germany
Linked well with van Hooijdonk, until the Dutchman threw his toys out of the pram.

Sub: Dariusz 'Jacki' Dziekanowski Poland
For entertainment value alone, the Disco King deserves his place on the bench.

FROM POINTS TO PINTS

11 players who've run or owned pubs

1. David Hay was running a pub in Paisley when the call came to replace Billy McNeill as boss in July 1983
2. Billy McNeill
3. Bobby Lennox
4. Bertie Auld
5. Roy Baines the Keeper's Arms, Tranent
6. Dom Sullivan
7. Harry Hood
8. Tommy Gemmell
9. Frank McAvennie owned Maccas, now known as Hoops
10. Patsy Gallacher
11. Anthony Shevlane

> LUBO MORAVCIK WAS PAVEL NEDVED'S BOYHOOD HERO. THE BEST 33-YEAR-OLD SIGNING IN THE WORLD

GOALFEST!

Celtic's 11 highest-scoring wins

1. **11-0 v Dundee** 22 October 1895
2. **10-0 v Hamilton Accies** League Cup quarter-final, first leg, 11 September 1968
3. **9-0 v Dunfermline Athletic** 14 January 1928
   9-0 v Airdrieonians 26 October 1963
   9-0 v KPV Kokkola European Cup first round, first leg, 16 September 1970
6. **9-1 v Vale of Leven** 5 May 1891
   9-1 v Clyde 25 December 1897
   9-1 v Clyde 4 September 1971
   9-1 v East Fife 10 January 1931
   9-1 v Arbroath League Cup third round, 25 August 1993
11. **9-2 v Clyde** League Cup, 8 December 1898

GOOD SPORTS

11 players who excelled in other disciplines

1. Walter Arnott 1895
Competed in the Clyde Regatta.
2. Jim Welford 1897-1900
Middle-order batsman for Warwickshire in 1895.
3. Willie Maley 1888-97
Sprinter and SAAU 100-yards champion 1896.
4. John Kelly 1929-30
Goalkeeper and boxer who sparred with Scots welterweight champ Tommy Milligan.

5. Willie Cringan 1917-23
Scottish quoits champion of 1926.
6. Robert Fisher 1942
Cricket for County Durham.
7. John Mallan 1942-43
Amateur boxer.
8. Sean Fallon 1950-58
Won the Henry Cup for long-distance swimming in Sligo, in August 1947.
9. Jim Craig 1965-72
Long jumper. Once runner-up to future Olympic star Lyn Davies in a Glasgow University competition.
10. Peter Latchford 1975-87
Junior basketball star.
11. Roy Aitken 1972-90
Like Latchford, a dab hand with a basketball.

Sub: Pat Bonner 1978-94, 1994-95
Played Gaelic football for Donegal.

THE GREAT DIVIDE

11 Old Firm quotes

1. "The worst club match in the world, without a doubt". **Jim Craig**

2. "The ultimate experience". **John Collins**

3. "I am often asked how the Rangers team of today compares with Celtic's Lisbon Lions of 1967. I have to be honest and say I think it would be a draw, but then some of us are getting on for 60". **Bertie Auld**, speaking in 1993.

4. "You're exhilarated and nauseated all in one." **Tommy Burns**

5. "You need the balls of a rhinoceros to play in an Old Firm game," **Ian Durrant** said. **Murdo MacLeod** certainly had the right equipment…

6. "I only know the first two lines of *The Sash*, because after that we've usually scored." **Roy Aitken**

7. "There's nothing worse than sitting in the dressing-room at Celtic Park after a defeat, not a word being said, listening to them next door going mental." **Ally McCoist**

8. "A tirade of abuse ended with him (Jock Stein) calling me 'A big f***ing poof' – exactly the words I was to have hurled at me by Graeme Souness ten years later. So at least the Old Firm view of me from the two sides of the fence was consistent". Ex-ref **Davie Syme** enjoys a warm reception.

9. "Both clubs soon saw the financial advantages in playing each other in games where the ethnic edge was clear-cut, and it was this commercialism, which the amateur sports writers of the day found repellent, that led to the two clubs being branded 'The Old Firm' in a *Scottish Referee* cartoon of 1904." Author **Bill Murray**, *The Old Firm In The New Age.*

10. "After five years of Rangers victories in the league, Celtic fans would have seen the club sold to the Ayatollah Khomeini if it gave a glimmer of hope of success on the park". **Michael Kelly**, former Celtic director, *Paradise Lost*, 1994.

11. "I know what it's like to be called an Orange bastard or a Fenian bastard, even though I've never been religious. There is real hate in these people's eyes. I don't like going to Old Firm games because of it. They turn my stomach". **Jackie McNamara**

GREAT HEADLINES

Read all about it

1. Bairns won, Bhoys out
Falkirk beat Celtic in the 1997 Scottish Cup semis and *The Sun* has a field day.

2. Supercaley go ballistic, Celtic are atrocious
Inverness Caledonian Thistle dump the Bhoys out of the Scottish Cup as John Barnes discovers the true meaning of "90 minutes of sheer hell". *The Sun*, again.

3. Celtic sign blank Czech
The *Daily Record* greets the arrival of Dr Jozef Venglos with a degree of understatement, 18 July 1988.

4. Joke Brown
The *Daily Record* welcomes the appointment of Jock Brown as general manager.

5 All hail, McPhail
The *Evening Times* salutes Billy McPhail's hat-trick in the 7-1 win over Rangers in the 1957 Scottish Cup final.

6. Modest Murdoch a true lionheart
Obituary for Bobby Murdoch, the *Daily Telegraph*, 16 May 2001.

7. Old Firm's Fireworks
The *Evening Times's* Saturday pink after the 4-4 draw at Ibrox on 22 March 1986.

8. An orgy of crudeness
The *Glasgow Herald* is unimpressed by Rangers's strong-arm tactics in Celtic's 4-0 Scottish Cup final win of 1969.

9. Barnes and the Emerald Eyal
The Independent on Sunday previews Barnes's challenge, 25 July 1999.

10. Celtic seek true messiah
The Sunday Times, 13 February 2000. Verily we say unto you, it wasn't John Barnes.

11. How can you tell Kenny's in trouble? By his spotty nose
A touch of surrealism from the *Daily Mail*, 11 February 2000.

GREAT WHITE HOOPS, SORRY HOPES

Here are the news

1. **Roy Aitken** the new Duncan Edwards
2. **Joe Carruth** the new Jimmy McGrory and the new Jimmy Quinn!
3. **Henry Callachan** the new Alec McNair
4. **John Colrain** the new Billy McPhail
5. **Dariusz Dziekanowski** the George Best of Poland
6. **Willie Fernie** Scotland's Stanley Matthews
7. **Peter Mackie** the new Kenny Dalglish
8. **George McLaughlan** the new Sandy McMahon
9. **Tony Shepherd** the new Bobby Evans
10. **Hughie Smith** the new Patsy Gallacher
11. **Derek Whyte** the new Billy McNeill

HAIR'S APPARENT

11 salon defectives

1. Jonathan Gould's dyed effort
"It wasn't until I saw myself on TV that I realised how stupid I looked," he said. What, so no one saw fit to mention it to you before?

2. Charlie Nicholas
You're not Bono, sonny. And as for those leather kecks…

3. Henrik Larsson
Behind his phenomenal goalscoring record, the Swede was probably best remembered for the distinctive dreadlocks he sported for much of his time at Celtic.

4. Alan Rough
OK, it was a more sensible job by the time he passed through Parkhead, but that bubble perm he took to Argentina in the 1978 World Cup should never have made it back through customs.

5. Neil Lennon
The midfield hard man arrived sporting his natural ginger look, but soon experimented with vivid platinum blond. It certainly made him stand out, but these days he's returned to his roots.

6. Johnny Doyle
His frizzy mop was one of the more distinctive Parkhead hairdos during the late 1970s. RIP.

7. Danny McGrain
It's not so much the world's greatest right-back's hair that's memorable. It's his beard. He wore it almost all his Celtic career and still has it today. Caused a bit of a stir in clean-shaven Tirana on the 1979 European Cup jaunt.

8. Frank McAvennie
Famous for his blond locks, but it takes fortnightly visits to the salon to maintain them. He's as ginger as Neil Lennon.

9. Regi Blinker
Just beat Larsson to the title of first man to combine dreadlocks with the green and white. Larsson wins the ability contest hands down.

10. Rudi Vata
What's the Albanian for mullet?

11. Davie Provan
See Alan Rough. The socks round the ankles were cool, though.

HIGH-SCORING SCRABBLE NAMES

Ks are only five, but that won't worry Brattbakk

1. **Dariusz Wdowczyk** 50 points
2. **Dariusz Dziekanowski** 50 points
3. **Jonas Kaduskeviechi** 39 points (aka John Jack, worth a respectable 26 points)
4. **Johannes Edvaldsson** 33 points
5. **Harald Brattbakk** 31 points
6. **Willie Kivlichan** 30 points
7. **Lubomir Moravcik** 30 points
8. **George McCluskey** 30 points
9. **Bobby Lennox** 27 points
10. **Francis Quinn** 26 points
11. **Joos Valgaeren** 24 points

HIGHEST-SCORING LEAGUE CAMPAIGNS AND LEADING SCORERS

Yeah, but before Larsson who was there, grandad?

1. 1915/16 116 (38 games) Charlie McColl (34)
2. 1935/36 115 (38 games) Jimmy McGrory bags 50, beating Steve Bloomer's world goalscoring record of 352 first-class strikes.
3. 1937/38 114 (38 games) Johnny Crum (24) and John Divers (20) lead the charge to a 20th title in Celtic's Silver Jubilee year
4. 1966/67 111 (34 games) Stevie Chalmers (23)
5. 1965/66 106 (34 games) Joe McBride (31)
6. 1967/68 106 (34 games) Bobby Lennox (32)
7. 2003/04 105 (38 games) Henrik Larsson (30)
8. 1926/27 101 (38 games) Jimmy McGrory (48)
9. 1930/31 101 (38 games) Jimmy McGrory (36)
10. 1938/39 99 (38 games) John Divers (17)
11. 2002/03 98 (38 games) Henrik Larsson (28)

HOOPS SPRING ETERNAL

11 other sides that look just like us

1. Portland Timbers USA
2. Santos Leguna Mexico
3. Shamrock Rovers Ireland
4. Sporting Lisbon Portugal
5. Västerås SK Sweden
6. Northwich Victoria England
7. Total Network Solutions League of Wales
8. Yeovil Town England
9. Rapid Vienna Austria, boo, hiss
10. Omonia Nicosia Cyprus
11. Leça FC Portugal

IF ONLY DIXIE DEANS HADN'T BALLOONED HIS PENALTY OVER THE BAR

IF ONLY…

11 flights of fancy

1. John Hughes hadn't struck the ball against Feyenoord keeper Eddie Graafland's legs in extra time in the 1970 European Cup final, with the score still at 1-1. With three minutes to go, Ove Kindvall won it for the Dutch side.

2. Dixie Deans hadn't missed his penalty in the 1971/72 European Cup semi-final shootout with Milan. Instead he ballooned it over the bar and the Bhoys bowed out. Ironically, in preparation at Seamill, he'd scored every time…

3. George McCluskey had put his shot between the posts, with the score goalless in the away leg of the 1979/80 European Cup clash with Real Madrid. McCluskey had been on target in the 2-0 first-leg win, but following this miss the Hoops capitulated 3-0 in the Bernabeu.

4. The 'bottle-throwing' incident against Rapid Vienna hadn't taken place, with the subsequent Viennese hullabulloo forcing a replay at neutral Old Trafford. "We felt that team could have gone all the way to the final," reflected a glum **Davie Provan**. To compound the misery, Vienna's winning goal in the third game came from a break after Roy Aitken hit a post.

5. Jock Stein had stayed at Celtic – where he'd been boss of the reserves since 1957 instead of leaving for Dunfermline Athletic in March 1960. Who knows what riches could have awaited in the early years of European competition?

6. Bobby Lennox's 'offside' goal against Liverpool in the 1965/66 Cup Winners' Cup semi-final second leg at Anfield had been given. It wasn't and Celtic were denied the chance to play in the final at… Hampden Park.

7. World War 2 hadn't broken out. And not only for altruistic reasons. Having finished outside the top three just once since 1929/30, Celtic's final places in the seven seasons after the full league programme resumed in 1946/47 read: seventh, 12th, sixth, fifth, seventh, ninth and eighth.

8. Jimmy McGrory, that greatest of Celtic goalscorers, had had more resources at his disposal on his appointment as manager after World War 2. Instead, with chairman Robert Kelly continually interfering with team selection, a mixture of promising young hopefuls – plus arrivals and departures – took the team to the brink of relegation in 1947/48. The ignominy! Celtic's greatest goalscorer is officially the club's worst manager – well, until John Barnes, anyway.

9. Our kamikaze defence had held its nerve against Partizan Belgrade in the 1989/90 Cup Winners' Cup, we wouldn't have been out of Europe after scoring five at home. But letting in the crucial late fourth meant we went out on away goals. "We climbed three mountains and preceded to throw ourselves off them," said **Billy McNeill**.

10. Dundee United had slipped up on the final day of the 1981/82 season. We stormed back from 2-0 down at the break to beat Rangers 4-2, but lost the title by a solitary point to the men from Tannadice.

11. Referee **Sbardella** of Italy hadn't been, in the words of Jimmy Johnstone, 'got at'. Instead a John Hughes strike against Dynamo Kiev was disallowed in the 1967/68 European Cup first-round clash and the holders' crown fell at the first defence.

INSPIRED COMEBACKS

Play to the final whistle, lads

1. Celtic 2 Internazionale 1 European Cup final, 25 May 1967
Referee Karl Tschenscher awards Inter a seventh-minute penalty after Jim Craig's foul on Cappellini, and the odds are on the Italians to lift the trophy. Think again…

2. Celtic 4 Rangers 2 21 May 1979
Trailing 1-0 after nine minutes, things look even more desperate when Johnny Doyle is dismissed for aiming a kick at Rangers's scorer Alex McDonald. But the ten men rally and Roy Aitken and George McCluskey help the Celts forge ahead. As the

pressure mounts, Rangers centre-half Colin Jackson heads past his own keeper and Murdo MacLeod's stunner delivers the title. "There are lots of fairytales throughout Celtic's history," says proud boss Billy McNeill. "And that was one of them."

3. St Mirren 0 Celtic 5 3 May 1986
Okay, from 1-0 to 4-0 up isn't strictly speaking a comeback, but the three goals in six minutes from Paul McStay (two) and Mo Johnston give Celtic the title on goal difference from Hearts. The Jambos had been top since the New Year and went into the final game two points clear, needing just a point. Two late Dundee goals from rabid Celtic fan Albert Kidd dashed their hopes.

4. Celtic 2 Dundee United 1 Scottish Cup final, 14 May 1988
United look like spoiling the centenary Double charge until Frank McAvennie bags two in the final quarter of an hour – the second with virtually the last hoorah.

5. Celtic 2 Hearts 1 Scottish Cup semi-final, 9 April 1988
The Bhoys stay on course for the centenary Double, scoring twice in the final three minutes to win. Mark McGhee and Andy Walker are the toast of Parkhead.

6. Celtic 2 Porto 3 UEFA Cup final, 21 May 2003
All right, so the Hoops lost. But Henrik Larsson's two textbook headers to level the scores as a defiant response to conceding really stir the blood.

7. Celtic 2 Dundee United 1 Scottish Cup final, 18 May 1985
Trailing 1-0 with 15 minutes left, Davie Provan and Frank McGarvey, with a late, late and miraculous bending header befitting the rubber man he was, win the day.

8. Celtic 3 Rangers 2 Scottish Cup final, 16 April 1904
The Celts are trailing 2-0 after just 12 minutes, but Jimmy Quinn's hat-trick, the last late on, wins the day and wins the striker a place in the record books.

9. Celtic 5 Sporting Lisbon 0 UEFA Cup second-round, second leg, 2 November 1983
Trailing 2-0 from the first leg in Lisbon, Sporting are swept away on a wave of attacks and five different names – Tommy Burns, Tom McAdam, Brian McClair, Murdo MacLeod and Frank McGarvey – go on the scoresheet. "They just collapsed, even though they were a good team," said a gobsmacked Davie Hay.

10. Celtic 2 Motherwell 2 Scottish Cup final, 11 April 1931
At 2-1 down with ten minutes left, Jimmy McGrory's goal looks a consolation – until Motherwell's Alan Craig heads the ball into his own net. The replay is won 4-2.

11. Celtic 2 Dundee 1 Scottish Cup final, 11 April 1925
A goal from ex-Celt Davie McLean looks to have won it for Dundee, but a mazy run
by Patsy Gallacher sees him upended in the box. Astonishingly, with the ball stuck
between his feet, he somersaults across the goal-line. The Dundee players' shock
at the outrageousness of it all results in Jimmy McGrory grabbing a second almost
immediately and an 11th Scottish Cup is won.

IT AIN'T HALF HOT, HUN

11 great Old Firm clashes

1. Celtic 4 Rangers 2 21 May 1979
The day ten men won the league – thanks to a goal from a Rangers's centre-half.
If everyone who claims to have been present had actually been there, the gate
would have been bigger than the population of China. Almost. Tragically, no TV
or radio coverage because of a union dispute.

2. Celtic 6 Rangers 2 27 August 2000
Martin O'Neill has his first Old Firm clash won within 12 minutes on an afternoon to
feature in any Bhoys' Own comic book fantasy. Henrik Larsson's stunner is still being
played out in countless back yards across the East End of Glasgow.

3. Celtic 7 Rangers 1 League Cup final, 19 October 1957
The biggest Old Firm win – and the largest margin of victory in British cup final
history. Celtic had not won the League Cup before 1956, but here they defended it
with awesome majesty. "We had joy, we had fun, we beat Rangers 7-1" (to the tune
of *Seasons In The Sun*) was still a firm playground favourite 20 years on.

4. Celtic 5 Rangers 1 21 November 1998
Lubo Moravcik's finest hour? The Slovak, fresh from MSV Duisberg, has Rangers
totally baffled, scoring twice on an afternoon in which he pulled more strings than
any symphony orchestra. Johan Mjallby also excels on his debut.

5. Celtic 2 Rangers 0 2 January 1998
A first league victory against Rangers in 11 attempts since 7 May 1995, and a crucial
step on the path to avoiding the 'ten-in-a-row' nightmare. The relief is tangible.

6. Celtic 1 Rangers 0 29 August 1987
A purring Billy McNeill describes this victory as "possibly the best football I have ever

seen in an Old Firm match". Praise indeed. Billy Stark's goal is the difference as Celtic claim a vital scalp on the way to the title – eventually won at a canter.

7. Celtic 5 Rangers 1 3 January 1966
Cigars all round – well, maybe that's not quite Jock Stein's style – but his first Old Firm clash at Parkhead since taking over is worth the extravagance. The Bhoys come back from a goal down to pulverise Rangers after the break. Stevie Chalmers takes the match ball for his hat-trick.

8. Rangers 4 Celtic 4 22 March 1986
Goals from Mo Johnston, Brian McClair and Tommy Burns put the Celts 3-1 to the good, only for McCoist, Fleck and McKinnon to put Rangers ahead. Murdo MacLeod's blinding 25-yarder gets the Hoops out of jail, and for once both sets of fans go home happy. A surprisingly passionate encounter, given that the teams were seven and nine points behind leaders Hearts at the time, but coming up on the rails…

9. Rangers 0 Celtic 1 18 April 1981
Charlie Nicholas gets the only goal, but the win is far more clear-cut than the scoreline suggests. The composure of the team display leaves Rangers with the realisation that the chase for the title is over.

10. Rangers 2 Celtic 2 6 May 1967
Two Jimmy Johnstone goals – one a 25-yard screamer – sew up a second successive title and complete a first domestic Treble in front of 78,000. Nice. Just the European Cup final to go now….

11. Celtic 5 Rangers 0 Scottish Cup semi-final, 21 March 1925
The odds are heavily stacked against the Celts with Rangers headed for a third consecutive title, but two goals apiece from Jimmy McGrory and Adam McLean, and another from Alec Thomson, offer a defiant gesture.

IT'S A SHORT CAREER

11 players with other professions

1. Jim Craig dentist
The Lisbon Lion sat out the pre-season tour of North America in the summer of 1966 to do his finals at Glasgow University dental school. While still a player, he kept his hand in with stints on children's teeth in Glasgow Corporation clinics.

2. Giles 'Gil' Heron professional photographer
Jazzman Gil Scott-Heron's dad, you know. Played five games at centre-forward in 1951/52, having impressed on a trial after being spotted on the club's 1951 North American tour. Also a keen boxer and cricketer, and had two books of poetry published.

3. Frank Haffey encyclopedia salesman
The Hoops keeper not only flogged books door-to-door, but also became a cabaret performer in Australia.

4. Allen McKnight navvy
The big keeper helped construct the M25.

5. Jimmy McMenemy chairmaker

6. Ian Young apprentice industrial chemist

7. Frank Brogan chartered accountant

8. John Fitzsimons doctor
Patched the cuts and bruises of Scotland's 1978 World Cup squad.

9. Billy McPhail ladies' hairdresser and restaurateur

10. Charlie Shaw barker at Parkhead Cross Fair

11. Graham Barclay professional guitarist
Although he gave up the game in 1977 to concentrate on the gentlemen's outfitters he ran with his brother.

Sub: Bobby Collins cobbler
Fashioned a boot-strap for the 1950/51 season to protect Alec Boden's injured foot.

JAMMY MOMENTS

Winning is just a temporary loan from Lady Luck

1. Colin Jackson turns the ball past his own keeper at Parkhead in May 1979 and ten men win the league. The harder we work, the luckier we get.

2. Frank McAvennie is the recipient of a lucky rebound off David Narey and turns the ball home to complete the comeback against Dundee United in the 1988 Scottish Cup final. Landlord, make ours a double.

3. Billy McNeill calls correctly on the toss of referee Louis van Raavens' two-and-a-half guilder coin, after both legs of the 1969/70 European Cup clash with Benfica finish 3-0 in favour of the home side. Penalty shootouts hadn't been invented yet – the misery of Milan was still two years away.

4. Chris Sutton's 51-second opening goal in the 'Demolition Derby' of August 2000 is allowed to stand with the aid of two dubious refereeing decisions. Rangers's Rod Wallace has a perfectly good goal disallowed. Martin O'Neill appears to be enjoying the luck of the Irish in his first Old Firm battle.

5. Dundalk miss a gilt-edged chance in the 1979/80 European Cup second-round, second-leg clash at Oriel Park in the final seconds. With the score 0-0 and two away goals in the bag, this would have been the most ignominious defeat in Celtic's European history.

6. Celtic force a replay against **Clyde** in the fifth round of the Scottish Cup in 1888 because it's too dark. Trailing 1-0, the players complain that the delay caused by three Clyde players removing illegal cross-bars from their boots had made the conditions unplayable.

7. With the unthinkable – relegation – looming against Falkirk in 1948, the Hoops are awarded a last-minute penalty. **Willie Corbett** – ever-present all season – makes no mistake from the spot and the Bhoys are safe.

8. Danny McGrain scored just seven goals in 663 games, so a long-range effort really wasn't worth the bother. But in the 1980 Scottish Cup final his extra-time 'shot' is turned goalwards by George McCluskey. Rangers keeper Peter McCloy is wrongfooted and Celtic win the silverware.

9. Murdo MacLeod's shot cannons off Gaetano Scirea, curving up past Dino Zoff, and the Celts are 1-0 up against Juventus in the 1981/82 European Cup.

10. Winning the league on goal difference from **Hearts** in 1985/86. What were the chances of that?

11. Sean Fallon gets a tip-off from a local publican about a young Rangers fan by the name of Danny McGrain. He visits the McGrain household in May 1967 and when young Danny gets home from school, he makes him a Celtic player.

JOCK STEIN MOMENTS

They'll never see his like again

1. When he picked a tie, he wore it until Celtic lost.

2. Stein signed only one non-Scottish player for Celtic: Danish goalkeeper Martin Bent. The only non-Scot to figure in the nine-in-a-row side between 1965-74 was the Icelandic centre-half Johannes Edvaldsson – signed by Sean Fallon while Stein was convalescing after his car crash.

3. At the victory banquet in Lisbon, Stein sat poker-faced throughout, turning to say to a journalist:"Well, I don't know what they can expect us to do next."

4. Stein had a distrust of the BBC during his early years at Celtic Park. Perceiving an anti-Celtic bias, he dubbed the Beeb's leading Scottish broadcaster Peter Thomson 'Blue Peter'. Thomson never covered another Celtic home match.

5. During the 1984 miners' strike, Stein stopped to cram various notes into an NUM collection box outside a ground before a game.

11. JOCK STEIN'S FIRST CELTIC XI

John Fallon

Ian Young   Tommy Gemmell

John Clark   Billy McNeill   Jim Brogan

Stevie Chalmers   Bertie Auld
Bobby Murdoch   Bobby Lennox
John Hughes

The Big Man gets off to a memorable start with his first Celtic side beating Airdrie 6-0 at Broomfield on 10 March 1965.

6. At a training session while managing Dunfermline, team joker Jackie Sinclair called him Jock. Stein's riposte was swift. "I am the boss, not Jock. Remember that." He later called the player's father and told him to ram the point home.

7. On his first day's training with Celtic he gave every member of the squad a ball. The first day's training before that had been a cross-country slog.

8. He twice left the dugout to go into the crowd to help deal with disturbances – once at Ibrox and again at Stirling Albion.

9. The Celtic players regularly ate on a Saturday night at the Vesuvio restaurant. Stein would scrutinise the bill looking for excessive spending. On finding an order for a cigar he assembled the players to discover who was responsible and reprimanded the culprit, Tommy Gemmell, for his flamboyant behaviour.

10. Stein was a pioneer of the win bonus system. Amounts of between £500 and £1,000 were commonplace payments for success. Curiously, the remuneration for victory in Lisbon had not been agreed on beforehand. Even Stein, the most frugal of men, it seems could not put a price on that success.

11. At half-time during the 1968/69 European Cup second-round, first-leg clash with Red Star, Stein promised Jimmy Johnstone that he wouldn't make him go to Belgrade if Celtic scored four goals after the break. After Johnstone had kept his side of the bargain by scoring two and setting up two more, Stein tried to pressure him into changing his mind, claiming that the British Embassy wanted him to go to strengthen relations with Yugoslavia. Johnstone later admitted: "Before the second game, I kept out of his road for about three days until they were all safely away."

JOCK STEIN REMEMBERED

What they said of the Big Man

1. "John, you're immortal".
Bill Shankly's right on the money, gladhanding the Big Man after winning the European Cup

2. "Let's not beat about the bush. They were reluctant to give him full control because he was a Protestant."
Billy McNeill on Stein's protracted appointment as boss in March 1965

3. "I've got a vivid memory from 1965, when it was announced that he was coming back from Hibs, of Billy McNeill saying, 'Oh, that's fantastic. Wait and see how things change now.'"
John Divers on Stein's return to the fold

4. "Before Jock arrived, nobody thought of balancing the back four or getting the various aspects of the team to play with each other. There was none of that. Then Jock came in and started doing this fairly logically. I think everybody just thought, 'This is good. We'll go along with this.'"
Jim Craig on the Big Man's genius

"BEFORE JOCK ARRIVED NOBODY THOUGHT OF BALANCING THE BACK FOUR"

5. "You knew, going out there, what to do and what your team-mates had to do and invariably he gave you the feeling that if you did it properly you would win. Normally, that was the case."
David Hay on his belief in Jock's game plan

6. "I think he should have been a doctor or a psychologist. He knew people and because he knew

11. JOCK STEIN'S LAST CELTIC XI

Peter Latchford

Alan Sneddon   Andy Lynch
Johannes Edvaldsson   Roddie MacDonald

Roy Aitken   Ronnie Glavin   Peter Mackie

Tom McAdam   Mike Conroy   George McCluskey

Jock Stein's last Celtic XI,
v St Mirren, Love Street,
29 April 1978. L 1-3.

what made us tick he made us feel we were the best team in the world. He knew how to make us believe in ourselves."
Jimmy Johnstone

7. "He would confront people. He would have a square go if it was on. He was a big, strong guy; quite a fearsome character."
Keeper Ally Hunter

8. "Stein was the greatest manager to ever draw breath. As a football man, there was no one who came anywhere close to him. He eclipsed Shankly, Busby and all the other legends in the game. He was in a class of his own."
Former Rangers boss Jock Wallace is impressed

9. "It must have been a terrible drain on him over the years. And he was a man who didn't know the meaning of the word relaxation."
Billy McNeill

10. "Class is something you can recognise easily in managers, but it's very hard to define. Jock Stein had it. He got it from his stature, the way he spoke and through

the authority he commanded over his players and the media. If you could bottle what he had you'd make a fortune."
Andy Roxburgh

11. "The rapport we had with the supporters was unbelievable. Big Jock encouraged that. We had a rota system at Celtic Park. Everybody had their dinner dances, supporters' nights or quizzes. There was always a minimum of three players at each of these functions."
Tommy Gemmell

JOINED AT THE HIP

11 memorable partnerships

1. Stevie Chalmers, Joe McBride, Bobby Lennox, Willie Wallace and Jimmy Johnstone

The all-conquering Hoops attack of 1966/67 crashed home 184 goals en route to glory in Lisbon. Stevie Chalmers and Joe McBride led the way with 36 and 35 respectively. McBride's tally was most remarkable as he didn't play after Christmas.

2. Bobby Lennox and Willie Wallace

They were the hot ticket in the 1967/68 title-winning season with 32 and 21 goals respectively. With 106 league strikes in all, the Hoops passed the century mark for a third season in a row.

3. Henrik Larsson and Chris Sutton

The Swede – top scorer in all but one of his seven seasons at Parkhead (the one in which he broke his leg) – found the perfect foil in the big Englishman. In the Treble-winning season of 2000/01, the prolific Larsson scored 53 to win the Golden Shoe, while Sutton played a crucial supporting role with 14. In 2003/04, the pair bagged 49 between them – close on half of Celtic's SPL record 105 strikes, Larsson getting 30, Sutton 19.

4. Charlie Nicholas and Frank McGarvey

The former, still 18, all style and swagger, the other possessed of an Inspector Gadget-esque elasticity. Like *Hart To Hart*, when they met, it was murder. They plundered 57 goals between them in all competitions as the 1981 title came to Celtic Park.

5. Frank McAvennie and Andy Walker

Local lads Frank and Andy racked up 50 goals between them in the centenary Double-winning season of 1987/88. Walker got the lion's share with 32.

6. Roy Aitken and Derek Whyte

At the other end of the pitch they were the cornerstones of a defence breached a miserly 23 times in 44 games – the meanest in Britain that season – and the club's best since 1921/22.

7. Joos Valgaeren and Johan Mjallby

Unpassable kingpins during the Treble year, the pair conceded just nine league goals all season as Celtic's goal difference read +81.

8. Charlie Shaw, Alec McNair and Joe Dodds

The keeper and his trusty right and left-back combo let in just 14 in 38 games on the way to the 1913/14 Double.

9. Jorge Cadete, Paolo Di Canio and Pierre van Hooijdonk

Just one season together – in 1996/97 – and there was nothing to show for it either, but when it was good, it was very, very good.

10. Johnny Crum and John Divers

Who says old football is rubbish? The forward pairing that shot the Hoops to the 1937/38 title would have given any defence a major migraine.

11. Jimmy Quinn, Peter Somers, Alec Bennett, Jimmy McMenemy and Davie Hamilton

The 1906/07 attack, which notched 80 goals, was as good as the backline of Sunny Jim Young, Willie Loney, Alec McNair, Jimmy Hay and Jimmy Weir.

KNOW YOUR HISTORY (1)

11 pre-war Celtic greats

1. John Thomson 188 appearances (1926-1931)
His death at 22 – the result of head injuries received in a clash with Rangers's striker Sam English – made him a legend. But his goalkeeping skills alone would have done that – he was already Scotland's national keeper, as renowned for his safe handling and remarkable composure as his bravery. More than 30,000 people attended his funeral in his native Fife. One league championship, two Scottish Cups.

2. Alec McNair 604 appearances, 11 goals (1904-25)
The Icicle was an integral part of the six-in-row title side between 1905-10, and picked up a further five league winners' medals between 1914-19. A Scottish Cup winner at 39 in 1923, he's also the oldest player to turn out for the club, aged 41 years and four months. Twelve league championships, six Scottish Cups.

3. Dan Doyle 123 appearances, five goals (1891-99)
In the days before professionalism the left-back was a controversial figure for receiving wages from Celtic – he got them a year early on the QT. Three league championships, three Scottish Cups.

4. 'Sunny' Jim Young 392 appearances, 13 goals (1903-17)
Converted from centre-back to right midfield – a genius switch by Willie Maley. Part of the six- and four-in-a-row sides between 1905-10 and 1913-17, he was called 'a glutton for work'. His nickname was an ironic comment on his dour disposition, but his loyalty was as good as it gets. Ten league championships, five Scottish Cups.

5. Sandy McMahon 217 appearances, 177 goals (1890-1903)
Maley said 'Duke' was the best header of a ball he'd seen – praise indeed. Good on the ball and with a fearsome shot, he was also known for his blistering pace and power. Four league championships, three Scottish Cups.

6. Johnny Campbell 215 appearances, 113 goals (1890-95, 1897-1903)
A man out of time, Campbell's close control and reading of the game was streets ahead of those around him. He matched striking partner Sandy McMahon's brace in the Celts' first trophy success – the 1892 Scottish Cup – and won another title and two Scottish Cups in his second spell with the club after winning the league with Aston Villa. Two league championships, four Scottish Cups.

7. Jimmy Quinn 331 appearances, 217 goals (1900-1915)
Willie Maley firmly believed Quinn – who played on the wing for the first three years of his Parkhead career - was "the greatest centre-forward we have ever possessed". You can't argue with the stats – a hat-trick in the 1904 Scottish Cup final win over Rangers cemented his folk-hero status. Brave, quick, strong, good in the air – he had everything a target-man needs. Six league championships, four Scottish Cups.

8. Jimmy McColl 169 appearances, 123 goals (1913-20)
What The Sniper lacked in height at 5ft 7in, he made up for with a deadly eye for goal. A permanent fixture in the four-in-a-row side between 1913-17, he topped 20 league goals for three consecutive seasons. Four league championships, one Scottish Cup.

9. Jimmy McMenemy 515 appearances, 168 goals (1902-20)
Known as Napoleon for his organisational skills – his passing, heading and shooting abilities were also something to see. A cornerstone of the side that won ten league titles between 1905-17, he saw the pitch as a chessboard. According to his boss Willie Maley, "he seldom, if ever, troubled himself with the physical side of the game – he had no need". Also coached the club, winning his first nine games in charge in 1934/35. Ten league championships, six Scottish Cups.

10. Patsy Gallacher 464 appearances, 192 goals (1911-26)
Announced his credentials as an 18-year-old with a goal in the 1912 Scottish Cup final against Clyde and never looked back. Known as The Mighty Atom or the Tiny Bit o' Grit for the phenomenal strength of his 5ft 7in frame. One of the great entertainers, he loved to take bigger men on – and usually won. Six league championships, four Scottish Cups.

11. Jimmy McGrory 445 appearances, 468 goals (1921-37)
His eight goals in the 9-0 walloping of Dunfermline Athletic on 14 January 1928 is the record individual scoring feat in Scotland and is unlikely to be broken. Supreme in the air – he got a third of his goals that way – he also had few peers on the deck. He set countless scoring records – he bagged 50 goals in 1935/36 and

was the Celts' top marksman in 12 of the 13 seasons between 1924-37. Three league championships, four Scottish Cups. Astonishingly, he only took a size six boot.

Sub: Johnny Crum 211 appearances, 87 goals (1932-42)
Alongside John Divers and Malky MacDonald, Crum was part of a forward line described as "tricky as a colony of monkeys". His frail 5ft 7in frame meant he had to be one step ahead of stronger opponents, and he usually was, thanks to his remarkable positional play.

KNOW YOUR HISTORY (2)

11 post-war Celtic greats

1. Pat Bonner 641 appearances (1978-94)
No-one had ever looked all that steady in nets for Celtic – even Ronnie Simpson, custodian for Celtic's finest hour-and-a-half in Lisbon, had been discarded by Jock Stein while at Hibs. It was clear this youngster from Donegal hadn't joined to make up the numbers. Within a year of arriving – as Jock Stein's last signing – he'd ousted Peter Latchford as first choice. His debut, appropriately enough, came on St Patrick's Day 1979, a 2-1 success over Motherwell. The following season he didn't miss a game, one of five ever-present campaigns in his Parkhead career. "Scottish goalkeepers are supposed to be bad enough, but an Irish keeper in Scotland… I just had to go out and try and prove everyone wrong," he said. He was as good as his word. Four league championships, three Scottish Cups and one League Cup.

2. Danny McGrain MBE 663 appearances, seven goals (1967-87)
A childhood Rangers fan, McGrain emerged as part of the 'Quality Street Gang' of talent in the post-Lisbon Lions years and soon became part of the Parkhead furniture. A tigerish tackler, he was rarely caught out of position and regularly lent a hand on the overlap. The length of his career was all the more remarkable given his series of injuries (including a head injury) and the diabetes he was diagnosed with in 1974. Six league championships, five Scottish Cups and one League Cup.

3. Tommy Gemmell 418 appearances, 63 goals (1961-71)
Tommy Gemmell and his flamboyant attacking instincts were brought to the fore in Celtic's finest hour. It was Big Tam, running on to the ball outside the Inter box, who thrashed home the equaliser in Lisbon in 1967 – he managed to repeat his scoring feat in the 1970 final. His shots were regularly measured at 70mph-plus – and his attendant armoury of power, pace and endless energy made him a key

figure for a decade. Six league championships, three Scottish Cups, four League Cups, one European Cup.

4. Billy McNeill MBE 790 appearances, 35 goals (1958-75)
Up there with Jock Stein in the Mr Celtic category, Caesar was a craggy centre-half who knew no fear yet rarely mixed it – just one sending-off in his career is testimony to his sense of fair play. The captain of the Lisbon Lions team, he led by example and could be relied on to pop up with a crucial strike when it was needed. It was his header that won Stein his first trophy (the 1965 Scottish Cup) and a similarly towering leap ushered Celtic through to the 1967 European Cup semi-finals against Vojvodina. Like Stein, he returned to serve the club he loved as a boss, never letting the side down in the process and winning eight trophies in nine seasons. Nine league championships, seven Scottish Cups, six Scottish League Cups, one European Cup. "He's my voice out on the park," said Stein. Enough said.

5. Roy Aitken 672 appearances, 53 goals (1972-90)
A man after boss Billy McNeill's own heart, Aitken's ferocious determination at centre-back established him in the Celtic Double-winning team of 1977/78 while still a teenager. So indispensable were his services, he was still there a decade later in the centenary Double-winning side. He could also play a neat game in midfield. "Feed the bear" they sang. How he feasted. Six league championships, five Scottish Cups and one League Cup.

6. Paul Lambert 275 appearances, 19 goals (1997–)
The only modern-day Celt to have tasted European Cup success (with unfancied Borussia Dortmund in 1997), Lambert was back in his native Glasgow within six months of lifting the trophy in a £2m move. Unruffled, unfussy and always composed, his skills at the base of midfield are not the kind that quicken the pulse but are no less vital – evidenced by four league titles in the past six years. Was made Celtic captain in 2001/02. Four league championships, two Scottish Cups, two League Cups.

7. Jimmy Johnstone 515 appearances, 130 goals (1961-75)
The flying flea (as a French journalist dubbed him) took an almost sadistic pleasure in torturing defenders, jinking this way, then that, then coming back for another go. Rarely has a player more typified the Celtic underdog spirit – Johnstone's impudence unsettled bigger, stronger opponents. At 5ft 4in, one of the club's shortest players, his reputation remains among the biggest. A former ballboy at Celtic Park, he built up his terrifying pace up by doing 100-yard sprints in his father's pit boots. Nine league championships, four Scottish Cups and five League Cups.

8. Paul McStay 677 appearances, 72 goals (1981-97)
Known simply as The Maestro, this Celtic Boys Club graduate made the top grade on both club and international stages – his 76 Scottish caps is a Celtic record. A goal on his Old Firm debut in October 1982 (the week after his 18th birthday) brought him to wider attention – where he stayed. A key member of the 1987/88 centenary Double winners, he became the third member of his family (after grandfather Jimmy and uncle Willie) to skipper Celtic in January 1990. Also captained Scotland at the 1992 European Championships. Two league championships, four Scottish Cups, one League Cup.

9. Bobby Murdoch 484 appearances, 102 goals (1959-73)
Converted from striker to midfielder, Fat Boab (as he was affectionately known) knew exactly where the frontmen wanted the ball and exploited it to the full. A crucial cog in the Lisbon Lions, Murdoch sprayed the ball regally around the park for more than a decade; Jock Stein allowed him to move south of the border only because "he had run out of challenges". Strong as an ox but with a a delicate touch, he proved equally popular at Middlesbrough, whom he helped to promotion in 1973/74. Seven league championships, four Scottish Cups, four League Cups, one European Cup. He was the first of the Lisbon Lions to die, from a stroke in 2001.

10. Bobby Lennox MBE 589 appearances, 273 goals (1961-80)
An uncanny ability to predict where a loose ball would bounce in the box, allied with scintillating close control, devastating pace and astounding fitness, made the 'buzzbomb' a key part of Celtic under Jock Stein – and kept him in the Parkhead picture until 1980. He resisted overtures from Arsenal to move south of the border to stay with the club he loved – and that loved him equally in return. Nine league championships, six Scottish Cups, four League Cups and one European Cup.

11. Henrik Larsson 315 appearances, 242 goals (1997-2004)
A player for all seasons, the Swede's arrival – Wim Jansen's first signing – created few headlines. He was soon enough making them himself, raining in headers, volleys and stunning free kicks from all angles, as if possessed by some supernatural force. Larsson topped the scoring charts at Parkhead in six of his seven seasons. Surely only a horrific double fracture of his leg against Lyon in the Champions League clash in November 1999 – he still has an alloy rod running the length of his shin – prevented him doing so in the 1999/2000 campaign. Remarkably, he was even better on his return after injury – the goal in the 6-2 Demolition Derby of August 2000 is one of the best Parkhead has seen. 2001/02's 53-goal effort in the Treble-winning season won him the Golden Shoe as Europe's top marksman. Four league championships, two Scottish Cups, two League Cups.

LITTLE-KNOWN FACTS ABOUT THE 1967 EUROPEAN CUP WIN

Hitch-hikers, gnashers and bonuses

1. Ronnie Simpson kept the players' false teeth in a bag at the back of his goal. The bag was nearly lost in the aftermath of victory.

2. Stevie Chalmers's winner was Celtic's 200th goal in all competitions that season.

3. Despite Jock Stein's noted fondness for win bonuses over wages, the team had not discussed the value of their reward before the game.

4. As Inter tried to spy on Celtic's training session the night before the European Cup final, Jock Stein got wind of the ruse and told his players to swap their usual positions – Jimmy Johnstone moved to centre-half.

5. During the preparatory week at Largs, Stein and his team sat down to watch a re-run of the 1960 final between Eintracht Frankfurt and Real Madrid.

6. Planning to travel to Glasgow to catch the Old Firm derby in a jet belonging to a millionaire friend, Inter boss Helenio Herrera had invited Stein to fly back with him to watch the Inter-Juventus game in Turin the following day. When he arrived, he told Stein that the offer was no longer good as he'd had to travel in a smaller plane, the seats of which would be too small for Stein. Stein had taken care not to cancel his existing arrangements to fly out to Turin. When he got there, the courtesy car organised by Herrera didn't materialise.

7. Coach Sean Fallon predicted the scoreline in his newspaper column that week.

8. As the players lined up to walk out on to the pitch, Bertie Auld led a chorus of *The Celtic Song* to unsettle the Italians.

9. John Lawrence, owner of Rangers, was at the airport to welcome the team home.

10. Ronnie Simpson had been supposed to collect the cup with Billy McNeill but was too emotional to go up.

11. Bobby Murdoch's brother hitch-hiked to Lisbon to see the game.

LOCAL HEROES

The European Cup-winning team all came from within 30 miles of Glasgow. Here's an alternative 11 of Glasgow-born Hoops

1. Denis Connaghan
2. Danny McGrain
3. Jim Brogan
4. Tommy Boyd
5. Pat Crerand
6. Tommy Burns
7. Paul Lambert
8. Murdo MacLeod
9. Jimmy McGrory
10. Bobby Evans
11. Bobby Collins
Sub: Frank McGarvey

LOOKALIKES

Didn't I see you in Scooby Doo?

1. Tommy Gemmell Danny Kaye
2. Wim Jansen Leonardo Da Vinci's Renaissance Man sketch
3. Henrik Larsson Jamie Oliver
4. John Colquhoun Bobby Ball
5. Bertie Peacock Paul Whitehouse
6. Denis Connaghan John Noakes
7. The young Jimmy Johnstone Mick Hucknall
8. Jock Stein Perry Mason played by Raymond Burr
9. Vidar Riseth Shaggy from *Scooby Doo*
10. Ramon Vega actor Anthony Sher
11. Chris Sutton Rupert Everett

MIDDLE MEN

11 unusual middle names of Celtic players

1. Paul **Marcellus** Elliott
2. John **Wotherspoon** Gilchrist
3. Thomas **Breckenridge** Craig
4. Samuel **Little** Glasgow
5. Gerald **Padua** McAlloon
6. Thomas **Valley** McGinlay
7. David **Prophet** McLean
8. Robert **McWilliam** McMillan
9. Robert **Haynes** Smith
10. Thomas **Earley** Stewart
11. Murdo **Davidson** MacLeod
Sub: George **Horsburgh** Allan

MOST-CAPPED PLAYERS

Kings of the passport stamps

1. **Pat Bonner** 80, Republic of Ireland
2. **Paul McStay** 76, Scotland
3. **Tom Boyd** 66, Scotland
4. **Danny McGrain** 62, Scotland
5. **Roy Aitken** 50, Scotland
6. **Henrik Larsson** 49, Sweden
7. **Kenny Dalglish** 47, Scotland
8. **Bobby Evans** 45, Scotland
9. **Johann Mjallby** 40, Sweden

10. John Collins 32, Scotland
11. Billy McNeill 29, Scotland

MOST-SATISFYING VICTORIES

Any win's a pleasure, but some are even better...

1. Celtic 2 Internazionale 1 European Cup final, 25 May 1967
Eighty years after Brother Walfrid founded a team to help feed the poor, comes
a story we can dine out on for the rest of our days.

2. Celtic 2 St Johnstone 0 8 May 1998
Cheerio, ten -in-a-row…

3. Celtic 6 Rangers 2 27 August 2000
Television pictures show an edgy bunch of orcs as O'Neill's men prepare to battle
like dogs of war before showing a fine artist's touch in sight of goal. After the dark
days of the 1990s it's clear O'Neill, like Brian Clough, is no respecter of reputations.

4. Celtic 4 Rangers 2 21 May 1979
Two goals in the last five minutes snatch the title from the Huns in one of the most
exhilarating finishes in the world, ever. Ten men, own goals, long-range screamers –
it's all here. It almost makes up for Thatcher coming to power two weeks earlier.

5. St Mirren 0 Celtic 5 31 May 1986
Three goals in six minutes win the title from Hearts, against whom Dundee
supersub – and rabid Hoops fan – Albert Kidd is simultaneously doing the business
with a double whammy. You couldn't make it up.

6. Rangers 0 Celtic 3 29 April 2001
Moravcik inspired, Larsson's 50th goal… What better way to put the finishing
touches to preparation for the last leg of the Treble than doling out the biggest
Old Firm spanking at Ibrox since August 1971?

7. Celtic 5 Rangers 1 21 November 1998
Lubomir Moravcik – look upon his works, ye mighty, and despair.

8. Celtic 7 Rangers 1 League Cup final, 19 October 1957
The biggest ever victory margin in a British cup final – and the largest in an

11. MARTIN O'NEILL'S FIRST CELTIC TEAM

Jonathan Gould

Alan Stubbs   Stephane Mahe
Joos Valgaeren   Tom Boyd

Jackie   Paul Lambert   Eyal Berkovic   Stilian
McNamara   Petrov

Henrik Larsson   Chris Sutton

The team that lined up against Dundee United at Tannadice on 30 July 2000 - Martin O'Neill's first match as manager ended in a 2-1 win.

Old Firm clash. Terry Jacks's *Seasons In The Sun* gets a reworking for a 1970s terrace smash.

9. The Coronation Cup 1953
Celtic, struggling dreadfully in the post-war years, see off Arsenal, Manchester United and Hibs (then the dominant Scottish force), with a 2-0 win in the final, thanks to Neil Mochan and Jimmy Walsh. A certain Jock Stein, at the heart of the Celtic defence, is integral to the success, a catalyst for the following season's league and Scottish Cup Double – the first in 40 years.

10. Rangers 0 Celtic 2 27 August 1994
A strange choice perhaps, but a win at Ibrox in the 1990s was about as rare as rocking horse doo-doo. Heroes on this occasion were John Collins – God bless the Predator boot – for his blinding free kick and Paul McStay.

11. Celtic 1 Motherwell 0 Scottish Cup final, 1951
The Hoops' first appearance in a domestic final since 1938 sees John McPhail – an injury doubt in the build-up – get the only goal after 13 minutes. Spookily appropriate timing – it was the club's first silverware in 13 years.

NO LOVE LOST

11 grudges we love to nurse

1. Rangers
How long have you got?

2. Hearts
What's wrong with these people? The Gorgie Road gargoyles haven't even the dignity to observe a minute's silence.

3. Porto
For those histrionics in the UEFA Cup final. You may be the darling of the English meejah, Mourinho, but you've forfeited our respect.

4. Manchester United
For pinching Paddy Crerand and Joe Miller, and some bad-tempered testimonials down the years.

5. Dunfermline Athletic
For the spineless capitulation that handed Rangers the 2002/03 title.

6. Atletico Madrid
For the brutal victimisation of Jimmy Johnstone in the 1973/74 European Cup – on and off the pitch. If that wasn't reason enough, we then had to play them behind closed doors in 1985. And they knocked us out again.

7. Motherwell
Seem to have a hoodoo over the Hoops – can anyone else explain the events of 21 May 2005?

8. Racing Club
For their antics in the 1967 World Club Championship. They have no place in football.

9. Airdrie
Rubbish, but always up for a scrap.

10. Rapid Vienna
For the play-acting in the European Cup Winners' Cup clash of 1984/85. You're a disgrace to the hoops.

11. Rangers Reserves
Well, you never know who might be in there…

ODDS AND SODS

11 unclassifiable bits of Celtic trivia

1. 144 eggs, 12 chickens, butter, tea, fruit, soup, fruit juice, steaks – the inventory of the food taken by Celtic 2,500 miles to the European Cup Winners' Cup quarter-final second leg in Tblisi, 1966.

2. Ronnie Simpson represented Great Britain in football at the 1948 Olympics.

3. Willie Maley played under the pseudonym Montgomery for several games in the 1893/94 season. Professionalism had yet to be officially adopted in this era of amateurism. Draw your own conclusions.

4. The Scottish Cup tie with Kilmarnock scheduled to take place on 26 January 1901 was played as a friendly after a telegram to the referee reading "park playable" was received as "unplayable" – so he didn't turn up.

5. Celtic Park hosted the first-ever organised speedway meeting in Britain on 28 April 1928.

6. While Celtic were bagging seven against Stirling Albion at Celtic Park on 13 December 1958, the Bhoys reserves were putting nine past them at Annfield.

7. In exchange for a pennant before the European Cup tie in Tirana on 10 September 1979, the Partizan skipper gave Danny McGrain a book on Albanian architecture.

8. To honour Celtic's eight titles in a row between 1965-73, the players all wore No.8 on their shorts for the game against Clyde on the opening day of the 1973/74 season – a 5-0 victory.

9. David Hay kept his contact lenses a secret from his team-mates because he thought it might jeopardise his chance of a game.

10. Celtic keeper Joe Cullen, custodian in the club's first silverware success against Queen's Park in the 1892 Scottish Cup, survived an explosion in his works factory just months after joining. Boss Willie Maley said he was never the same again.

11. There is no television footage of Celtic's five second-half goals in the 1957 Scottish Cup final defeat of Rangers. A BBC technician went for his half-time cuppa and forgot to remove a dust cap from his camera after the break.

ONES THAT GOT AWAY

11 players we should have hung on to

1. Kenny Dalglish
The £400,000 Liverpool paid in the summer of 1977 may have been a British record, but it was still a steal. With his departure, it was only a matter of time before Jock Stein left too – the end of one era and the chance to begin the next gone with it.

2. George Connelly
Quit football at just 26. He'd been Footballer of the Year just three years earlier.

3. Shay Given
The Irish keeper slipped through our net, before keeping them out for Blackburn Rovers and Newcastle United.

4. Joe Jordan
The teenage Jaws, whose dad was a Celtic nut, was invited for trials, but Celtic passed. Jordan is the only British player to have scored in three World Cup finals.

5. Graeme Souness
Yes, the lord of Mordor trained with Celtic as a young Scots prodigy before moving to swinging London with Spurs.

6. Pat Crerand
It's still unclear today what happened during Crerand's move to Manchester United in January 1963. One minute he wanted to go, the next he wanted to stay, the next he'd gone. What was clear was that Celtic missed a trick – Crerand had already shown his mettle by giving the great Ferenc Puskas a real test at Celtic Park against Real Madrid.

7. Liam Miller
A Bosman transfer. A Hoops legend in the making now sitting in Manchester United's stiffs.

8. Brian McClair
Another steal. McClair had scored 99 times in 145 games when he left Celtic Park for Old Trafford for just £850,000 in July 1987.

9. Dunky MacKay
When the *Evening Times* polled its readers for the greatest Celtic side after the European Cup triumph, Dunky MacKay was a shoo-in at right-back. A stylish defender who was equally happy going forward, he was skipper before Billy McNeill took the armband in August 1963. He left just months before Jock Stein walked through the door.

10. Andy Walker
From Double-winning hero of 1987/88 to forgotten man by 1991. Emerged in England with Bolton Wanderers.

11. Lou Macari
A wrangle with Jock Stein over a £5 weekly rise prompted Lou to skip down to Old Trafford in January 1973.

ONE-GAME WONDERS

11 post-war blink-and-you-miss-'ems

1. Graham Barclay v Clydebank Scottish Cup, 15 February 1975, W 4-1
2. John Buckley v Arbroath League Cup, 1 September 1982, W 4-1
3. Charles Cairney v Raith Rovers 1 October 1949, D 2-2
4. Tom Curley v Hearts 26 September 1964, L 2-4
5. Bert Fraser v Hibernian 3 April 1948, L 2-4
6. John Gorman v Hamilton Academical League Cup, 25 September 1968, W 4-2
7. Philip Gormley v Aberdeen 10 January 1948, W 1-0
8. Joe Haverty v St Mirren 17 October 1964, W 4-1
9. Peter Lamb v St Mirren 31 August 1946, W 1-0
10. Ronnie Mitchell v Hearts 3 January 1948, L 0-1
11. William Morrison v Raith Rovers 12 January 1952, L 0-1

OUR BOYS

11 Celtic Boys Club graduates

1. Roy Aitken 483 appearances, 40 goals (1972-90)
2. George McCluskey 142 appearances, 55 goals (1973-93)
3. Mark Reid 134 appearances, 5 goals (1977-85)
4. Charlie Nicholas 187 appearances, 85 goals (1979-82, 1995-96)
5. Paul McStay 515 appearances, 57 goals (1981-97)
6. Peter Grant 364 appearances, 15 goals (1982-97)
7. Steve Fulton 76 appearances, 2 goals (1987-93)
8. Gerry Creaney 113 appearances, 36 goals (1987-94)
9. Mark McNally 122 appearances, 3 goals (1987-95)
10. Brian O'Neil 120 appearances, 8 goals (1989/97)
11. Aiden McGeady 27 appearances, 5 goals (2004 –)

OWN GOALS AND OTHER GAFFES

Own goals by us and others

1. Henrik Larsson's first goal at Celtic Park was memorable for all the wrong reasons – it was past his own keeper. More crucially, it looked like putting the kibosh on Celtic's 1997/98 UEFA Cup hopes at the first hurdle, as Larsson put Austrians SC

Tirol Innsbruck level on the night and 4-3 up on aggregate. The Swede had also gifted Hibs a winner on his league debut. Clearly the man was a liability…

2. Colin Jackson heads past Peter McCloy to hand Celtic the 1979 title crown.

3. East Fife's **Robertson** gets Celtic out of jail against the Second Division side in the 1927 Scottish Cup final. Adam McLean and Paddy Connolly complete a 3-1 win. Incidentally, the action is heard for the first time by a radio audience.

4. Tommy Gemmell's pass leaves John Clark stranded and Vojvodina Novi Sad score the only goal of the European Cup quarter-final first leg of March 1967. Billy McNeill ensures this one had a happy ending in the return at Parkhead.

5. Aberdeen centre-half **Willie Young** slices Neil Mochan's cross into his own net for the first in a 2-1 win for the Celts in the 1954 Scottish Cup final – the club's first Double in 40 years.

6. Keeper **Allen McKnight**'s punt upfield is intercepted by Eammon Bannon for Kevin Gallacher to score in the 1988 Scottish Cup final.

7. Rangers keeper **Henry Rennie** steps over his own line with the ball to give Celtic a draw in the 1909 Scottish Cup final.

8. Jim Craig brings Cappellini down in the box and the resulting penalty puts Celtic a goal down in the 1967 European Cup final.

9. Johnny Bonnar makes a pig's ear of a cross to give Clyde's Archie Robertson an equaliser direct from a corner in the 1955 Scottish Cup final. Celtic lost the replay 1-0.

10. Motherwell's **Alan Craig** is the toast of the Hoops after heading past his own keeper under pressure to make it 2-2 late on in the 1931 Scottish Cup final.

11. Frank Haffey tries to take a quick free kick to Dunky McKay, but succeeds only in putting the ball in his own net against St Johnstone in February 1962.

A WRANGLE WITH STEIN OVER A £5 WEEKLY RISE CAUSED LOU MACARI'S MOVE TO OLD TRAFFORD

PLAYING AWAY

11 Celts and their hobbies

1. William McStay
Bred pedigree dogs.
2. Frank McGarvey
Loves wildlife programmes.
3. Roy Aitken
A virtuoso pianist.
4. Johnny Hodge
A happy camper.
5. Anthony Shevlane
Collected antiques and second-hand books.
6. Eamon McMahon
Greyhound trainer.
7. Peter Somers
An accomplished pianist. Played to a packed house on the night of Jimmy Quinn's testimonial at St Mungo's Halls in 1907.
8. Graeme Sinclair
Elvis impersonator.
9. Desmond White
The former chairman had a passion for scuba diving and mountaineering.
10. Kenny Dalglish
Big Tamla Motown fan.
11. Martin O'Neill
As befits a law graduate, is fascinated by crime and often visits crime scenes in his spare time.

RIPPING YARNS

11 essential Celtic reads

1. *Not Playing For Celtic – Another Paradise Lost* **David Bennie** (Mainstream)
Often hilarious, brilliantly written tale of a Celtic fan's life with Parkhead as a
backdrop. As engaging as *Fever Pitch*.

2. *Fields Of Green – The Celtic Dream Team* **Roddy Forsyth** (Mainstream)
Fascinating memories with Nicholas, Provan, Bonner, McGrain, McNeill and others
recalling their most memorable matches for the Hoops.

3. *The Glory And The Dream – The History Of Celtic FC 1887-1986* **Tom Campbell**
and **Pat Woods** (Mainstream)
Rich, extensively researched history which illuminates the club's first 100 years.

4. *Celtic: The Jock Stein Years* **Graham McColl** (Chameleon)
Simple but effective picture-driven look at Stein's legacy, with eye-catching replica
souvenirs. A great gift for a junior Celt.

5. *An Alphabet Of The Celts: A Complete A-Z Of Celtic FC* **Eugene McBride**, **Martin
O'Connor** and **George Sheridan** (ACL/Polar)
Does exactly what it says on the Tin. Vital reading for any self-suspecting anorak.

6. *The Essential History of Celtic* **Graham McColl** and **George Sheridan** (Headline)
Whistle-stop trawl through the archives, with handy season-by-season at-a-glance
guide at the end. The 50 Best Players section should get people talking.

7. *One Afternoon in Lisbon* **Kevin McCarra** and **Pat Woods** (Mainstream)
McCarra and Woods skilfully take you to the heart of the action in Lisbon. So vivid,
you can feel the sun on your back.

8. *Celtic in Europe: from the Sixties to Seville* **Graham McColl** (Mainstream)
Engrossing blow-by-blow account of Celtic capers on the continent.

9. *The Head Bhoys: Celtic's Managers* **Graham McColl** (Mainstream)
From Maley to O'Neill, they're all here. Even John Barnes.

10. *Celtic: The Official Illustrated History 1888-1996* **Graham McColl** (Hamlyn)
Another incisive work by this Celtic aficionado.

11. *Willie Maley - The Man Who Made Celtic* **David Potter** (Tempus Publishing)
Potter breathes life into the man who helped make dreams reality.

ROGUES' GALLERY

People who should steer clear of dark alleys

1. Mo Johnston

Crossed himself to goad Rangers fans after being sent off in the 1986 Scottish Cup
final. Three years later he joined them from Nantes having reneged on an
agreement to re-sign for Celtic. Recently had to pull out of a veterans' match when
it was mooted that he might play a half each for Rangers and Celtic. "I won't go to
Rangers. They don't sign Catholics and anyway I don't want to go to Ibrox" (25 June
1989). "I think I can do a great job for Rangers" (26 days later on 21 July). A player
with everything except a sense of what's right.

> MO JOHNSTON WOULD CROSS HIMSELF TO DELIBERATELY GOAD RANGERS FANS

2. Jim Farry

The head of the Scottish Football Association
deliberately leaves Jorge Cadete's work permit
application in his drawer until the last few weeks of
the 1995/96 season. Farry is sacked and Celtic
receive £50,000 compensation, which is no
compensation for Rangers winning the league.

3. Rudi Weinhofer and Rapid Vienna

Weinhofer's play-acting in the 1984/85 European Cup Winners' Cup – claiming he
had been hit by a bottle thrown from the crowd – followed the sending-off of
centre-half Reinhard Kienast for lamping Tommy Burns. The Austrians' complaints to
UEFA eventually forced the second-round game to be voided. A second replay at
Old Trafford saw a clinical performance from Rapid as Celtic imploded.

4. Juan Carlos Lorenzo

Him and his Atletico Madrid team. Lorenzo had been in charge of the Argentinian side that disgraced itself in the 1966 World Cup against England. He'd honed his dark arts supremely in the years before the 1973/74 European Cup semi-final clash. Atletico had three men sent off and another five booked in the first-leg at Celtic Park, which finished 0-0. Even Eusebio clashed with Jimmy Johnstone and the resulting brawl required police intervention. Celtic's request for the return to be played at a neutral venue was ignored and the Spaniards won the second leg 2-0.

5. Racing Club

The play-off for the World Club Championship of 1967 saw four Celtic players dismissed in an orgy of violence, gamesmanship and over-excitable police carrying swords and batons. Bobby Lennox, Jimmy Johnstone, John Hughes and Bertie Auld all get their marching orders.

6. Scott McDonald

The Celtic fan who pooped the 2004/05 championship party with two goals for Motherwell.

7. Nicola Amoruso

The Juventus man tumbles under an innocuous challenge from Joos Valgaeren with the score at 2-2 in the Stadio Delle Alpi during the 2001/02 Champions League clash, then gets up and converts from the spot to give the Italians victory. Celtic fail to qualify for the second phase by one point.

8. José Mourinho

Him and his Porto prats in the 2002/03 UEFA Cup final. Step forward Derlei for goading the fans after scoring and then kicking the ball at Didier Agathe, and Nuno Valente, dismissed for upending Alan Thompson.

9. Andy Goram

The black armband worn at an Old Firm clash for the death of his aunt conveniently coincides with the passing of notorious UVF loyalist Billy Wright.

10. El-Hadji Diouf

Liverpool's Senegalese striker receives a two-match ban after spitting at Celtic fans in the 2002/03 UEFA Cup quarter-final first leg at Parkhead.

11. Bob Valentine

Having given Rangers the League Cup with a dubious penalty a few months earlier, here's our favourite ref again for the 1983/84 Scottish Cup final v Aberdeen. First he lets a suspiciously offside-looking goal by Eric Black stand, and then Roy Aitken is dismissed for a challenge on Mark McGhee. Booooo!

SAFE HANDS

11 Celtic keepers and their clean sheets

1. **Charlie Shaw** 227 (1913-25)
2. **Pat Bonner** 172 (1978-94, 1994/95)
3. **David Adams** 100 (1902-12)
4. **Joe Kennaway** 75 (1931-40)
5. **John Thomson** 57 (1926-31)
6. **Ronnie Simpson** 54 (1964-70)
7. **Peter Latchford** 52 (1975-87)
8. **Frank Haffey** 41 (1958-64)
9. **Joe Bonnar** 40 (1946-58)
10. **Jonathan Gould** 36 (1997-2002)
11. **Evan Williams** 36 (1969-74)

SCANDALS

11 moments that left a nasty taste

1. Gathering dust
Jorge Cadete's work-permit application takes an unfeasibly long time to process at the business end of the 1995/96 season. As 'Farrygate' unravels, it transpires that Scottish Football Association head honcho Jim Farry has been letting it moulder away in his drawer. He is subsequently fired. Rangers win the league.

2. Dallas cowboy

During the crucial Old Firm clash on 2 May 1999, referee Hugh Dallas is hit by a coin after enjoying a pally exchange with Giovanni van Bronckhorst as Rangers prepare to take a corner. When the kick is taken Dallas blows for a penalty, when no clear infringement appears to have happened. Rangers score and go on to win 3-0. Dallas – who had four stitches for his pains – sends three off, books another ten and there are four pitch invasions. "The hardest game I've ever had to handle," he says.

3. You're a guy, Uruguay

The brawling that mars the World Club Championship is followed by rumours that Jock Stein has been dismissed. In a tremendously bad-tempered third match in Montevideo in 1967, Bobby Lennox, Jimmy Johnstone, John Hughes and Bertie Auld are all dismissed, along with two Racing players. The players are fined £250 each.

4. Half a dozen of the other

On the final day of the 2002/03 season, Rangers play Dunfermline needing to rack up a five-goal winning margin. Rangers win 6-1, taking the title by one goal. "We knew they'd lie down and they have done," says an emotional Chris Sutton.

5. The game in Spain

On the eve of the 1973/74 European Cup semi-final second leg with Atletico Madrid, Jock Stein and Jimmy Johnstone receive death threats. "What chance have they got of hitting you when you get out there and start joking and jiving? I can't move, I'm sitting there in that dugout." The words of Stein, ever alert to the prospect of using anything to hand as a pep talk. Atletico won 2-0, with 1,000 police swelling the gate.

6. Cheers

Following the 1980 Scottish Cup final, Celtic and Rangers are served with £20,000 fines for supporters' skirmishes on the field. As a result, the Criminal Justice (Scotland) Act subsequently makes it illegal to drink at Scottish games. Back at the football, George McCluskey's goal wins it for the Bhoys.

7. Fairytales

Frank McAvennie and Rangers players Chris Woods, Terry Butcher and Graham Roberts all appeared in court after an incident during the Old Firm clash of October 1987. McAvennie, who was found not guilty of his part in the disturbance said: "It was like Goldilocks and the three bears."

8. Hot off the press

During his first spell as Celtic boss, Billy McNeill had several run-ins with journo and

11. SCOTTISH LEAGUE CUP WINNERS

Dick Beattie

John Donnelly   Sean Fallon

Willie Fernie   Bobby Evans   Bertie Peacock

Charlie Tully   Neil Mochan
Bobby Collins   Sammy Wilson
Billy McPhail

The team that memorably beat Rangers 7-1 to lift the Scottish League Cup at Hampden Park on 19 October 1957.

professional irritant Gerry McNee. The pair traded blows on a European trip to Hungary (after which McNee mysteriously sported a black eye), and McNeill blanked him at a press conference. Celtic chairman Desmond White carpeted his boss and read out a club statement which ran: "You can rest assured that Mr McNee will be accorded all the normal press facilities in future."

9. Senseless waste
As the 1909 Scottish Cup final between Celtic and Rangers finishes with no extra time evident, angry fans invade the pitch, battling police, starting fires and stoking them with whisky. Both clubs are forced to pay £150 in compensation to hosts Queen's Park and the Cup is withheld. Hope it wasn't malt whisky…

10. Tightwads
Having turned down a move to Arsenal in 1928 to stay with his beloved Hoops, Jimmy McGrory, unknown to him, was then paid less than his team-mates for the next decade. What a shabby way to treat a legend.

11. Amateur hour
In 1891 Everton left-back Dan Doyle, fresh from winning the league as a professional

with Everton, switches to Celtic – still supposedly amateur. The Football League, smelling a rat, blacklists the Bhoys on the grounds of breach of contract.

SCOTTISH FOOTBALL WRITERS' PLAYERS OF THE YEAR

11 darlings of the media

1. **Billy McNeill** 1965
2. **Ronnie Simpson** 1967
3. **Bobby Murdoch** 1969
4. **George Connelly** 1973
5. **Danny McGrain** 1977
6. **Charlie Nicholas** 1983 (also PFA Young Player of the Year 1981, 1983)
7. **Brian McClair** 1987 (also PFA Player of the Year)
8. **Paul McStay** 1988 (also PFA Player of the Year, 1983 PFA Young Player of the Year)
9. **Craig Burley** 1998
10. **Henrik Larsson** 1999, 2001 (also PFA Player of the Year for both those seasons)
11. **Paul Lambert** 2002

Sub: Chris Sutton 2004

SEASON'S GREETINGS

11 Celtic topscorers in a Scottish league season

Figures only refer to league goals
1. **Jimmy McGrory** 1935/36 (50)
2. **Jimmy McGrory** 1926/27 (49)
3. **Jimmy McGrory** 1927/28 (47)
4. **Henrik Larsson** 2003/04 (35)
5. **Brian McClair** 1986/87 (35)
6. **James McColl** 1915/16 (34)
7. **Bobby Lennox** 1967/68 (32)
8. **Joe McBride** 1865/66 (31)
9. **Henrik Larsson** 2001/02 (30)
10. **Charlie Nicholas** 1982/83 (29)
    Henrik Larsson 1998/99, 2001/02 (29)

SEASONS IN THE SHADE

11 campaigns that are best forgotten

1. 1977/78

Jock Stein's last stand. With McGrain injured and Dalglish on his way out in search of greater things, the Bhoys struggle to 36 points. A young, inexperienced side – average age only 22 – flirts with relegation before rallying to fifth place, 19 points adrift of Rangers. There's also the disappointment of a second-round European Cup exit to Austrians SW Innsbruck. The lowest league finish since 1965 and a tearful end to a glorious era that brought 25 trophies in 13 years.

2. 1999/2000

And now on Celtic TV, it's John Barnes's Football Nightmare… The Hoops finish second, 21 points behind Rangers. Larsson smashes his leg up, Inverness Caley Thistle enjoy their finest hour. All this and Rafael Scheidt too.

3. 1979/80

Four defeats in five games in April – including two to Aberdeen – see the Dons take the title by a point come May. The on-field violence – mounted police are called in – that mars the jubilant scenes after George McCluskey's goal against Rangers in the Scottish Cup final is likened to something out of *Apocalypse Now*. Steady on…

4. 1994/95

Fourth spot, 18 points behind Rangers. In exile at Hampden Park and beaten in the League Cup by Raith Rovers in a penalty shootout. Celtic win the Scottish Cup without conceding a goal, but even then it's via a dour 1-0 success over Airdrie.

5. 1993/94

Lou Macari is next through the revolving door following the departure of Liam Brady in October. The excitement of beating Young Boys of Berne with an own goal for a 1-0 aggregate win in the UEFA Cup is tempered by the arrival of Carl Muggleton and Wayne Biggins. Fourth place in the league, a League Cup semi-final defeat by Rangers and dumped straight out of the Scottish Cup by Motherwell.

6. 1991/92

Brady's bunch finish third as Rangers win a fourth consecutive title. Celtic sign Tony Cascarino for £1.1m and suffer their worst European kicking ever at the hands of Neuchatel Xamax, who beat the Hoops 5-1.

11 SASSENACHS XI

Peter Latchford

Lee Martin · Alan Stubbs
Tony Mowbray · Paul Elliott

Alan Thompson · Tommy Johnson · Steve Guppy

Andy Payton · Chris Sutton · Ian Wright

Sassenachs. A coachload of southern softies who have played for the Hoops.

7. 1988/89

A 5-1 defeat against Rangers in August sets the tone and another 4-1 Old Firm drubbing on 3 January is followed in March by Frank McAvennie's departure to West Ham United. Mo Johnston's decision to sign for Rangers instead of returning to Celtic Park is the nadir and a symbol of the shift in Scottish dominance to Ibrox.

8. 1989/90

Oh dear. Not only are Rangers 17 points better than Celtic as they trail home in fifth, the Hoops are ten points worse off than runners-up Aberdeen. The Dons, with Slick Nick up front, beat the Celts 9-8 in a Scottish Cup final penalty lottery, and also knock the team out of the League Cup at the semi-final stage.

9. 1947/48

Twelfth place, 23 points behind title-winners Hibs. News that football has resumed after the war doesn't seem to have hit home – the Bhoys finish 12th, the club's lowest league finish ever. Luckless boss Jimmy McGrory has to field three keepers in one match against Dundee. Yes, it was that bad.

10. 1952/53
A third consecutive fewer-points-than-games season. Here, 29 from 30, to be exact.

11. 2004/05
It promised so much, but as we went to press, it was lying in tatters. Martin O'Neill quitting, defeat snatched from the jaws of victory at Fir Park. Can we talk about something else now, please?

SEASONS IN THE SUN

Ain't it great to be alive?

1. 1888/89
OK, there's no Rangers, no league programme and Shettleston and Cowlairs are staging posts on the road to Hampden. This was Celtic's first season – reaching the Scottish Cup final just nine months after forming was an astonishing achievement. And the Bhoys also won the North-Eastern Cup, beating Cowlairs 6-1.

2. 1892/93
Celtic take their first Scottish League title, pipping Rangers by a point.

3. 1904/05
Rangers are beaten in a play-off for the title – the first in seven seasons and the first of six successive championships under the stewardship of Willie Maley.

4. 1906/07
It takes eight Scottish Cup ties to see off Clyde, Morton, Rangers and Hibs, but Hearts are beaten 3-0 in the final, making it the first domestic Double by a Scottish club. It's also the third of six consecutive titles with marksmen Quinn, Jimmy McMenemy, Peter Somers and Alec Bennett peppering the target.

5. 1913/14
A third league and Cup Double – but there's a 40-year gap before the next one. Still, it's the first of another four consecutive league titles…

6. 1953/54
Neilly Mochan, Willie Fernie and Bobby Collins top the shots as Jimmy McGrory's Bhoys win a first post-war championship and take the Scottish Cup.

7. 1966/67
Having won the league and League Cup and reached the Scottish Cup final, plus a semi-final of the European Cup Winner's Cup in his first full season, Jock Stein ups the ante. Celtic win all three domestic trophies, the European Cup and the Glasgow Cup, just for good measure. The best season in the world, ever.

8. 1978/79
Stein has gone but Billy McNeill returns to steer Celtic to a last-gasp title against Rangers – with that 4-2 win over the old enemy to seal it.

9. 1987/88
A league and Scottish Cup Double. What better way to celebrate your centenary, managed by the most successful skipper in club history, Billy McNeill, back for a second spell in the Parkhead hot seat?

10. 1997/98
No ten-in-a-row for Rangers as Wim Jansen makes amends for being part of the Feyenoord 1970 European Cup-winning side that beat Celtic.

11. 2000/01
Martin O'Neill's first season ends with a glorious Treble and a top-flight record of 97 points (there'll be a new record of 103 points along in 12 months), 15 ahead of second-placed Rangers. Larsson leads the way with 53 goals in all competitions. He bags a brace in the League Cup final win over Kilmarnock and the Scottish Cup final success over Hibs on his way to the Golden Shoe.

SHIPS THAT PASSED IN THE NIGHT

11 players who nearly signed for Celtic

1. Rivaldo
After a will-he-won't-he saga in the summer of 2004, he didn't, and joined Olympiakos instead. "How dare Martin O'Neill ask Rivaldo to go for a trial in America? That is an insult to my client and football. People will be crying tears of laughter when they hear Celtic wanted to take Rivaldo on trial." That'll be a no from Rivaldo's agent Carlos Arime, then.

2. Johnny Carey
Celtic beat old Bhoy Scott Duncan, manager of Manchester United, to the signing

of Benny Gaughran, but Duncan had the last laugh when he snapped up one of the post-war game's greats.

3. Eddie Gray
Celtic offered a £3,000 signing-on fee in 1962, but he opted for Don Revie's Leeds United instead.

4. Alfredo Di Stefano
A frantic August 1964 was spent chasing the Spanish legend with the lure of a one-year deal. Somehow he found the rarefied air of Glasgow something he could live without. The fact that he'd already signed for Espanyol instead didn't deter Jimmy McGrory and languages graduate John Cushley haring around after him with a cheque for £30,000 for a year's work.

5. David Ginola
It's hard to escape the impression that we were used as leverage in the deal that took him to Newcastle United. He wasn't worth it…

6. Dwight Yorke
In talks with the Hoops until the last minutes of the 2004 summer deadline, Yorke finally opted for Birmingham City. A narrow escape for us, judging by his time in the Midlands.

7. Marcel Desailly
Celtic made a last-ditch move for the World Cup winner after he left Chelsea in 2004, but to no avail.

8. Taribo West
Dunfermline Athletic accused the Hoops of trying to scupper their attempts to sign the Nigerian international centre-half with a name like an American tower block. In the end he joined neither.

9. Gordan Petric
Dundee United's eccentric Croatian centre-half was a target for Tommy Burns, who was incensed by his decision to move to Rangers instead.

10. Graeme Sharp
Having signed Murdo MacLeod from Dumbarton in 1978, Billy McNeill passed up the chance to take a future Everton legend.

11. Gareth Southgate
Rumours of a summer transfer were never substantiated. He eventually left Aston Villa for Middlesbrough.

SHIRT SHIFTERS

11 significant Celtic kits

1. 1888
The first Celtic strip – white shirts, green necks and a Celtic cross on the left breast.

2. 1903/04
Celtic swap to the hoops. They first see action against Third Lanark.

3. 1935/36
The first strip to have a collar (white). Previously shirts had round necks.

4. 1960/61
A friendly match against Sparta Rotterdam sees the Bhoys sport numbers on their shorts for the first time.

5. 1968/69
Experiments with different designs for away kits see an all-white number used for various matches.

6. 1984/85
The first sponsored kit. On 27 September, the Hoops run out to meet Dundee in shirts bearing the logo of local glazing firm CR Smith, who also sponsor Rangers. Fans are not impressed, but the money finances the purchase of Mo Johnston from Watford for a Scottish record fee of £400,000.

7. 1992/93
The association with CR Smith is broken and the Hoops are adorned with the logo of Ford dealer, Peoples.

8. 1996/97
A black-and-luminous-yellow hooped away shirt – reminiscent of Borussia Dortmund's eye-catcher, just not as good.

9. 2001/02
Umbro are slammed by fans when the kitmakers announced they are to break with the club's famous hooped design, with gaps under the arms.

10. 2003/04
A new sponsorship deal starts with Carling. As with previous contracts with CR Smith and NTL, the brewers also sponsor Rangers. The deal underlines the popularity of the Old Firm – parent company Adolph Coors know the two teams will assist their bid to break into the Scottish market.

11. 2005
The Daily Record publishes exclusive pictures of Celtic's new Nike kit. Sadly for the paper, the images turn out to be fakes knocked up by a 15-year-old schoolboy in Ballymena!

SHORTEST NAMES

11 players whose surnames had four letters, or fewer

1. Jamie Bell
2. Alfie Conn
3. Jim Bone
4. Tom Boyd
5. Davie Hay
6. Johnny Crum
7. Andy Bell
8. Willie Cook
9. Chris Hay
10. William Gray
11. Stuart Gray

SLEEPING WITH THE ENEMY
11 PLAYERS WHO TASTED LIFE ON BOTH SIDES OF THE OLD FIRM

And a couple of near misses...

1. Mo Johnston
Celtic 1984-1987, Rangers 1989-91

2. John Dowie
Rangers 1969-72, Celtic 1977-79

3. Tom Sinclair
Six games on loan from Rangers in 1906/07

4. Alfie Conn
Rangers 1967-74, Celtic 1977-79. The only man to win a Scottish Cup final with both clubs.

5. Tom Dunbar
Rangers 1891, Celtic 1892.

6. Scott Duncan
Rangers 1913, Celtic loan 1919.

7. Mike Galloway
Spent eight weeks training with Rangers as a teenager.

8. James McPherson
Rangers (loan) 1885, Celtic (loan) 1890.

9. James Young
Celtic (loan) 1918, Rangers 1918.

10. Ian Young
Celtic 1961-68, trained at Ibrox as a teenager.

11. Murdo MacLeod
Rangers missed out on his signature as a teenager. Ha ha ha!

SONGS TO LEARN AND SING

11 Parkhead staples (lyrics available at TalkCeltic.net)

1. The Fields Of Athenry
Faux Irish, but stirring nonetheless.

2. Over and Over

3. Celtic Celtic
Ode to the Lisbon Lions.

4. You'll Never Walk Alone
Nicked from Liverpool in the 1960s, but sung much better. Belted out immediately before the kick-off of every game (even when the PA system is trying to play the mandatory Champions League tune on Euro nights).

5. The Boys Of The Old Brigade

6. Hail Hail
(For It's a Grand Old Team)

7 The Johnny Thomson Song
Ode to our tragic goalkeeper

8. The Wild Rover

9. This Land Is Your Land

10. We Shall Not Be Moved

11. Oh Hampden In The Sun

SOUND THRASHINGS IN EUROPE

11 European pastings by the Bhoys

1. **Celtic 9 PV Kokkola 0** (Finland) 1970/71 European Cup
2. **Celtic 8 Suduva Marijampole 1** (Lithuania) 2002/03 UEFA Cup
3. **Celtic 7 Jeunesse Esch 0** (Luxembourg) 2000/01 UEFA Cup
4. **Celtic 7 Waterford United 0** (Ireland) 1970/71 European Cup
5. **Celtic 7 Valur Reykjavik 0** (Iceland) 1975/76 European Cup Winners' Cup
6. **Celtic 6 Go Ahead Eagles 0** (Holland) 1965/66 European Cup Winners' Cup
7. **Celtic 6 Cwmbran Town 0** (Wales) 1999/2000 UEFA Cup
8. **Celtic 6 Diosgyori 0** (Hungary) 1980/81 European Cup Winners' Cup
9. **Celtic 6 Jeunesse Esch 0** (Luxembourg) 1977/78 European Cup
10. **Celtic 5 Basel 0** (Switzerland) 1963/64 European Cup Winners' Cup
11. **Celtic 5 Sporting Lisbon 0** 1983/84 UEFA Cup

In four European games against Celtic, Luxembourg's Jeunesse Esche have conceded 22 goals and scored one.

SUPER STUBS

11 touted tickets and the going rate

1. **Internazionale, European Cup final, 1967** £200-£400
2. **Feyenoord, European Cup final, 1970** £100-£175
3. **Dinamo Batumi (away), Cup Winners' Cup, 1995** £150-£200
4. **Racing Club, World Club Championship, 1967** £100-£200
5. **1960s European home matches** £50-£75
6. **Valencia (away), Inter-Cities Fairs Cup, 1962/63** £100-£150
7. **Go Ahead Deventer (away), Cup Winners' Cup, 1965/66** £100
8. **Dukla Prague (away), European Cup, 1966/67** £100-£150
9. **Dynamo Kiev (away), European Cup, 1967/68** £50-£75
10. **Red Star Belgrade (away), European Cup, 1968/69** £75-£125
11. **St Etienne (away), European Cup, 1968/69** £75

TALKING A GOOD GAME

11 ex-players turned pundits

1. Charlie Nicholas
A mainstay of Sky's Soccer Saturday panel. Has lost none of his rakishness.

2. Pat Crerand
Anchorman at Manchester United's MUTV. Loved Celtic so much he's spent 40 years in Manchester.

3. John Collins
A Sky regular. Also commentates on Scotland games.

4. Mick McCarthy
The ex-Eire and current Sunderland boss appears regularly on Sky and the BBC.

5. Kenny Dalglish
Stints with Sky, BBC and Scottish Television.

6. Murdo MacLeod
BBC Scotland.

7. John Barnes
Now host of John Barnes's Football Night. We've already seen John Barnes's football nightmare, thanks. If you do switch it on, you'll be astonished to discover that he's actually found something he's worse at than being a manager.

8. Paul Elliott
Frequent contributor to BBC Scotland's Celtic coverage, especially on big European

11. TREBLE-WINNING XI

Rab Douglas

Johan Mjallby   **Ramon Vega**   **Joos Valgaeren**

Alan Thompson
(Tommy Johnson)

Didier Agathe

Neil Lennon   **Lubomir Moravcik**
(Jackie McNamara)

Paul Lambert
(Tom Boyd)

Chris Sutton   **Henrik Larsson**

The side that beat Hibernian 3-0 in the Scottish Cup final at Hampden Park on 26 May 2001. In so doing, Celtic claimed the Treble.

nights. Was also a regular on Channel 4's Under the Moon (including one extremely drunk Hogmanay effort) and Italian football coverage.

9. Davie Provan
A Sky regular.

10. Alan McInally
Another Sky Soccer Saturday staple.

11. Andy Walker
1980s hero works for both Radio Clyde and Scottish Television.

TERRACE WISDOM: 11 INSPIRED CHANTS

Sing up at the back there

1. "When we're in Seville, you'll be watching The Bill"
Sending the message out loud and clear to our chums at Mordor.

11 TITLE-WINNERS WHO PIPPED RANGERS'S TEN-IN-A-ROW

Jonathan Gould

Tom Boyd   Enrico Annoni
Marc Rieper   Alan Stubbs

Jackie McNamara   Craig Burley
Paul Lambert   Phil O'Donnell
(Morten Wieghorst)   (Harald Brattbakk)

Henrik Larsson   Simon Donnelly
(Regi Blinker)

The team that beat St Johnstone 2-0 at Celtic Park on 9 May 1998 winning the title and, crucially, preventing Rangers from winning ten-in-a-row.

2. "Cheerio, ten-in-a-row"
Can you feel the relief even reading the words?

3. "Rambo's got a hard-on"
Alan McInally loses his composure ogling the Celtic cheerleaders.

4. "Feed the bear"
Popular words of encouragement for Roy Aitken.

5. "Bobo's gonna get ye, Bobo's gonnae get ye"
Plain and simple for our teak-tough centre-half.

6. "He's fat, he's round, he's worth a million pounds, Mark McGhee"
Everyone does it now, but it was good in the mid-1980s.

7. "Dixie, Dixie, Dixie!"
Just three days after he balloons his spot-kick high into the sky against Milan, Dixie Deans walks off the pitch with his name ringing in his ears.

8. "Michael Fagan shagged the Queen"
Ode to the July 1982 Buckingham Palace security-breacher. One for the active sectarian, perhaps.

9. "Heeeeeeeey baby/ooh aaah/I wanna knooooooow/Who the f*** is Flo?"
Well, he was never going to get a song from them, was he?

10. "Cheer up Craig Levein/Oh what can it mean/To a fat Jambo bastard/and a shit football team"
Belted out to the tune of *Daydream Believer*.

11. "You are my Larsson/My Henrik Larsson/You make me happy when skies are grey/We went for Shearer/But he's a wanker/So please don't take my Larsson away"

THANK GOD FOR…

The names that made us great

1. Andrew Kerins
Aka Brother Walfrid, without whom…

2. Hibernian
Six of the first Celtic team that played Shettleston in the club's first Scottish Cup tie were poached from them.

3. Jock Stein
For cooling his interest in Wolves to take the Celtic job at the third time of asking on 9 March 1965. He'd been offered the post first as Sean Fallon's right-hand man, then as joint manager.

4. Cycling
The 1897 World Cycling Championships funded ground improvements at Celtic Park thanks to a donation of £500 from the Scottish Cycling Union. The club became a limited company on the back of the proceeds.

5. Willie Maley
Served the club until he was 71.

6. Pantelic, Vojvodina Novi Sad's keeper
With an hour gone in the 1966/67 European Cup quarter-final second leg, Celtic were drawing a blank and heading out of the tournament. That's when Pantelic dropped Tommy Gemmell's cross for Stevie Chalmers to equalise.

7. Tommy Burns
Although his three-year reign brought only one trophy, he did instigate the group huddle we know and love today.

8. Wim Jansen
Although his time was short, it was long enough to bring Henrik Larsson to the club. He has his place in history ring-fenced forever for that – and for preventing the dread spectre of Rangers's ten-in-a-row.

9. Hoopy the Huddle Hound
For bringing a much-needed tonic in the early months of the 1997/98 season.

10. Henrik Larsson
Quinn, McGrory, Johnstone, Lennox, Dalglish, stand aside. The greatest of the great. Defied injury to return twice the player.

11. Martin O'Neill
"I'm a bit of a dreamer, but I'm also a realist," he mused on his appointment in June 2000. He has made those dreams come true. The natural successor to Jock Stein as Celtic's top dog. We'll never see the likes of the Lisbon Lions again, but 80,000 Celts in Seville means he did something right.

THINGS YOU'LL PROBABLY NEVER SEE AGAIN
Rub your eyes as hard as you like, they actually happened

1. Four penalties in a game
Willie Ferguson is on his way to immortality with five goals against Dundee in Celtic's record 11-0 victory, 1885/96.

2. A Celtic committee man sitting in on piano for the Rangers Glee Club
John McLaughlin was wont to in the 1880s.

3. Six hundred cartloads of snow being removed before a league match

On 29 January 1910, that's how many trips it took before the game at St Mirren could go ahead. Celtic lost 2-4.

4. Two games in a day
On 15 April 1916, Celtic warmed up for the 3-1 win at Motherwell with a tidy 6-0 win over Raith Rovers at home in the afternoon.

5. The same penalty missed three times
Well, nearly. In a league match against Hamilton Academical on 10 November 1917, Joe Dodds's spot-kick – and two subsequent rebounds – were saved.

6. Three goalkeepers in one game
In the League Cup encounter with Dundee on 6 September, 1947, Willie Miller went off after 11 minutes to be replaced by full-back Bobby Hogg. After he too got crocked, centre-forward Joe Rae took over the goalkeepers' gloves. Perhaps not surprisingly, Dundee won 4-1.

7. Two goals from the same corner
Having just netted directly from a corner-kick against Falkirk on 21 February 1953, Charlie Tully was forced to take the kick again – with the same outcome.

8. A 6-5 scoreline
Aye, that's how it finished when Celtic met Leith on 30 March 1894.

9. Rangers and Celtic fans fighting – not each other but the police
The Hampden Riot of 1909 erupts after the Scottish Cup final is drawn 1-1 and there's no extra-time.

10. Celtic playing eight games in 11 days
In the 1908/09 season, the Hoops won five and drew two of the games played between 19 and 30 April en route to defending the title by a point from Dundee. It was the fifth championship for the six-in-a-row side between 1905 and 1910.

11. A player turning out for a Sunday side
Centre-forward Willie Crilly was a regular for Glasgow Meat Market outfit the Pale Ale in the 1920s.

THREE AND IN

11 hat-trick heroes

1. Jimmy McGrory

Eight – that's eight – goals against Dunfermline Athletic, 1928. He'd twice scored four in a game and nabbed two further hat-tricks while still only 20. The first three against the Pars came in the opening nine minutes. They don't make 'em like that anymore.

2. Jimmy Quinn

Celtic 3 Rangers 2, 1904 Scottish Cup final. It was the first hat-trick in a final and all the sweeter because Rangers had been 2-0 up. Ironically, The Equator (so-called because he was always at the centre of things) only got the nod because first-choice Alec Bennett was considered to have been tapped up by Rangers. Quinn repeated the feat against Rangers on 1 January 1912.

3. Stevie Chalmers and Bobby Lennox

Five goals each as the highest Celtic score in 73 years is racked up. It finishes 11-0 against Hamilton Academical in the League Cup quarter-final, first leg at Celtic Park on 11 September 1968. The second leg is a more conservative 4-2 win, giving a fairly comfortable aggregate score of 14-2.

4. Dixie Deans

Six of the best in the 7-0 pulverising of Partick Thistle on 17 November 1973.

5. Dixie Deans

Again. Deans deserves a separate entry for his feats against Hibs alone. Boy, did he have it in for the men from Easter Road – his 18 goals in 13 outings included three hat-tricks, two in finals. The first, in 1972's 6-1 Scottish Cup final mauling, adds his name to Jimmy Quinn's in the record books as the only other man to score a hat-trick in a final. The hat-trick in the slightly closer 1974 League Cup win (6-3) was preceded by another three in a 5-0 league success the previous weekend.

6. Jacki Dziekanowski

Surely the only man who scored four and still finished on the losing side. That'd be enough to make anyone go out on the booze, not that he needed any excuse. Jacki's quartet came in an astonishing night of Euro action against Partizan Belgrade at Parkhead. The Cup Winners' Cup, second-round, second leg win finished 5-4 in our favour, but we still went out on away goals.

7. Harry Hood
Three against Rangers in the League Cup semi-final at Hampden on 5 December 1973. Harry was the last Celt to score a hat-trick against Rangers. My, that's a long wait.

8. Bertie Auld
Five against Airdrie at Broomfield in the Scottish Cup, 10 March 1965. The first signing of Stein's reign puts his weight squarely behind the new man.

9. Jock Weir
A recent £7,000 arrival from Blackburn Rovers, Jock repays his fee straight off the bat at the end of the 1947/48 season. His hat-trick against Dundee in a 3-2 win spares us the unthinkable – relegation.

10. Bobby Collins
Kept his nerve three times from the spot against Aberdeen on 26 September 1953.

11. John Hughes and John Divers
Get three each against a hapless Airdrie in a 9-0 Parkhead romp on 26 October 1963. Hughes also got five in an 8-0 rout of Aberdeen in January 1965.

WILLIE CRILLY WAS A REGULAR FOR GLASGOW MEAT MARKET OUTFIT THE PALE ALE

UNIVERSITY CHALLENGE

11 Celtic brainboxes

1. Jim Craig
Craig missed 1966's pre-season US tour to sit dentistry finals at Glasgow University. He claimed Stein never warmed to him because he wasn't working-class enough.

2. Brian McClair
He was in the second year of a maths degree at Glasgow University when he signed for Celtic in June 1983.

3. Leigh Richmond 'Dick' Roose
Doctor of bacteriology and goalkeeper who played one game in 1910. A wealthy eccentric who, while with Aston Villa, hired a train to get him to the game on time.

4. Andrew Davidson
Medical student at Glasgow University. Played for the Hoops between 1913-14.

5. Thomas Bogan
The winner of Stow College of Printing's John Wylie Silver Medal, no less! Played for the Hoops between 1946-48.

6. John Cushley 1960-67
MA in modern languages from Glasgow University.

7. Alex Kiddie 1944/45
BSc from St Andrews University.

8. Willie Kivlichan 1907-11
MA from Glasgow University.

9. Matt Lynch 1935-48
BSc from Glasgow University.

10. Joe Riley 1928-30
BSc from Glasgow University.

11. John Weir 1978-82
Studied civil engineering at Strathclyde University.

WATCHING YOU, WATCHING US

11 big-screen and TV moments

1. Ally McCoist in a Bhoys shirt? You betcha – with the aid of some computer magic, Ally plays a former Celtic player in 2000's straight-to-video effort *A Shot At Glory*. McCoist is Jackie McQuillan of Kilnockie FC (no, really) whose American owner wants to export the team to Ireland. Whaddya know, they win the cup and everything turns out great. What an ingenious plot twist! Worth seeing for Robert Duvall's appalling bash at Glaswegian.

2. In the 2004 movie *The Day After Tomorrow*, the chaps at the Scottish weather centre are watching the Hoops take on Manchester United during a US tour.

3. Veteran director Ken Loach is a collaborating on a new movie called *Tickets*, in which three Celtic fans are en route to Rome, with the aid of black-market tickets.

4. There's a bloke with a Celtic top on in the park in the 2003 movie *Three Blind Mice*.

5. Stilian Petrov's wedding was broadcast live on Bulgarian TV in June 2001.

6. *The Fields of Athenry* can be heard at the end of *Veronica Guerin* and it's also played by the piper on the pier in *Dead Poets Society*.

7. Is that the 1990s Hoops strip in a shop window during *Harry Potter And The Philosopher's Stone*?

8. *Erin Go Bragh* is belted out at the end of *American Pie 3*, should you feel the need to venture beyond the first two movies.

9. In recent Robert De Niro flick, *City By The Sea*, Bob shares his train carriage with a chap in a Celtic-crested woolly hat.

10. *Lord Of The Wing* – ace Jimmy Johnstone documentary.

11. Wet Wet Wet: Playing Away at Home – love is all around as the kings of MOR rock Celtic Park in 1997.

WEBSITES

Hoops in cyberspace

1. www.cfconline.co.uk
2. www.ntvcelticfanzine.com
3. www.lonestarceltic.com
4. www.rangersfansvcelticfans.com
5. www.bhoyfever.co.uk
6. www.keep-the-faith.net
7. www.celtic-mad.co.uk
8. www.jimmyjohnstone.com
9. ww.fridayclub.co.uk
10. www.celticquicknews.co.uk
11. www.etims.net

11. WHEW! THE XI THAT AVOIDED RELEGATION

Willie Miller

Bobby Hogg   Jimmy Mallan

Bobby Evans   Willie Corbett   Pat McAulay

Jock Weir   Johnny Paton
John McPhail   Willie Gallacher
Dan Lavery

The team that avoided relegation from Scottish League Division A on the final day of the season beating Dundee 3-2 at Dens Park on 17 April 1948.

WHAT THE LISBON LIONS DID NEXT

Destinations of the 1967 European Cup winners

1. **Ronnie Simpson** retired in 1970
2. **Jim Craig** joined Hellenic in 1972
3. **Tommy Gemmell** joined Nottingham Forest in 1971
4. **Bobby Murdoch** joined Middlesbrough in 1973
5. **Billy McNeill** remained at Celtic until his retirement in 1975, before returning as manager in 1978/79
6. **John Clark** joined Morton in 1971
7. **Jimmy Johnstone** joined San Jose Earthquakes in 1975
8. **Willie Wallace** joined Crystal Palace in 1971
9. **Steve Chalmers** joined Morton in 1971
10. **Bertie Auld** joined Hibernian in 1971
11. **Bobby Lennox** retired in 1980

WHAT THEY SAY ABOUT US

Quote unquote

1. *"Celtic was not just a football club to me, it was my life"* Sean Fallon

2. *"Are they really better than the Southamptons and Coventrys of this world?"*
Manchester United chairman Martin Edwards goes on the charm offensive when faced with the prospect of Celtic joining the Premiership, 1997

3. *"I think Celtic are as good as the best teams here in Italy".*
Milan coach Carlo Ancelotti clearly knows more about football than Martin Edwards

4. *"I can't wait to see my team play again. They're the greatest side in the world. I haven't been able to get to a match for years, but that will all change now ".*
Bishop Roddy Wright tells squeeze Kathleen McPhee the real reason for having eloped with her, 1996

5. *"Celtic is a love affair that we take to our deaths".*
Celtic rebel leader and board member Brian Dempsey, 1991. Dempsey failed in his bid to get the club moved to Robroyston

6. *"Celtic is like one big family and when we used to go to supporters' functions it was as if you were members of the family".* Tommy Gemmell

7. *"The greatest team on earth".*
A poster for a Celtic fixture in the Midlands in the 1890s leaves little room for argument

8. *"We can have no complaints. Celtic deserved their victory. We were beaten by Celtic's force. Although we lost, the match was a victory for sport".*
A magnanimous Helenio Herrera, Inter boss, salutes the Lisbon Lions

9. *"It will stick in my mind for ever that after the game the Celtic players were extremely good sportsmen and, together with their supporters, they gave us a standing ovation when we were receiving the cup".*
Eddy Graafland, Feyenoord keeper, after the 1970 European Cup final

10. *"I don't believe 50,000 fans will travel to Seville. That is madness. It is an exaggeration. I think a fair number will be around 4,000. We are talking about a final to be played on a Wednesday, a day when people normally work."*
The best-laid plans of UEFA security chief Rafael Carmine go slightly awry – 80,000

Celts turn up for the 2003 UEFA Cup final

11. *"There is surely something uniquely deluded about a persecution complex suffered by supporters of a club whose silverware haul is among the biggest in the world history of the game. But then that in itself is the source of the complaint; Celtic fans throughout the 1990s have provided the highly entertaining phenomenon of the glory-hunter whose club never wins anything. A century of sucking in prizes like a black hole, and then they hit a decade in which their trophy count is level with Raith Rovers and Motherwell."*
Chris Brookmyre, *The Absolute Game*

WIN OR LOSE, WE'RE ON THE BOOZE

11 Celtic pubs in Glasgow

1. **Bairds** Gallowgate, Glasgow
2. **Hoops** Gallowgate – used to be **Maccas**, owned at one time by Frank McAvennie
3. **Croy Tavern** Croy (near Cumbernauld)
4. **Bar 67** Gallowgate, Glasgow
5. **Sharkey's Bar** Hope Street, Glasgow
6. **Springfield Vaults** London Road, Glasgow
7. **McConnell's Bar** Hope Street, Glasgow
8. **McGinn's** Hope Street, Glasgow
9. **Kelly's Bar** Pollockshaws Road, Glasgow
10. **Celtic Supporters' Association** London Road, Glasgow
11. **Annie Armstrong's** Parkhead Cross, Glasgow

WONDER GOALS

Net-bulgers that produced the mightiest roars down the years

1. Henrik Larsson v Rangers 27 August 2000
The sun on our backs in Martin O'Neill's first Old Firm clash after ripping into Rangers with three goals in 12 minutes. Taking the ball from Sutton, Larsson beats Tugay, feints to the right, nutmegs Bert Konterman and advances before lobbing Stefan Klos to make it 4-1. Fifty-three goals in one season – and that was the best.

2. Brian McClair v Dundee United 18 August 1984
There's not a huge amount on when McClair picks up the ball in his own half, so he

keeps going. And going, and going. As the Tangerines's defence stands back, expecting a pass, he decides he may as well finish the job off, blootering the ball past Billy Thomson for the equaliser.

3. Frank McGarvey v Dundee United, Scottish Cup final, 18 May 1985
The rubber man's 'bendy' header beats Dundee United's Hamish McAlpine late on to give the Celts the 1985 Scottish Cup. First it curves out, then miraculously it curves inwards again to go in off the post.

4. Jimmy Johnstone v Rangers 6 May 1967
Jinky jinks, weaves and then unleashes a 25-yard belter to put Celtic 2-1 up at Ibrox with 15 minutes left and on course for a first domestic Treble.

5. John Hughes v Dynamo Zagreb, Cup Winners' Cup second round, first leg, 4 December 1963
Yogi proves he's smarter than the average bear all right, as he leaves the Dynamo defence for dead, sidestepping two of the Czechoslovakian World Cup final side from 1962 to put Celtic 1-0 up at Parkhead.

6. Davie Provan v Dundee United, Scottish Cup final, 18 May 1985
With time running out, the Hoops get a free kick. A trademark Provan strike is measured to perfection and beats the United wall for the equaliser.

7. Patsy Gallacher v Dundee, Scottish Cup final, 11 April, 1925
Floored by a Dundee defender after a mazy run into the penalty box, Gallacher jams the ball between his feet before somersaulting over the line to equalise. His teammates mob him – after disengaging him from the netting.

8. Bobby Hogg v Third Lanark, Glasgow Cup, 25 August 1936
Taking advantage of the blinding evening sunlight, right-back Hogg's 65-yard punt beats the Third Lanark keeper all ends up.

9. Jimmy McGrory v St Mirren, 1934 Scottish Cup fourth round
Jimmy meets Bobby Hogg's hoofed clearance from his own half on the edge of the 12-yard box to head past the keeper. Sadly, the goal is disallowed.

10. Tommy Burns v Dundee United, 22 April 1981
Burns sends the travelling faithful at Tannadice into paroxysms of delight as he beats two defenders before smashing the ball into the roof of the net to clinch the 1980/81 flag.

11. Tommy Gemmell v FC Zurich European Cup, first-round, first leg, 28 Sept 1966
Everyone knows *that* goal in Lisbon, but the 40-yard effort at Parkhead – the first of
the victorious campaign – was pretty darn special, too.

THE WRITE STUFF

11 Celtic autobiographies

1. **A Lifetime In Paradise** Jimmy McGrory
2. **Passed To You** Charlie Tully
3. **Fire In My Boots** Jimmy Johnstone
4. **All The Way With Celtic** Bobby Murdoch
5. **A Lion Looks Back** Jim Craig
6. **Hail Caesar** Billy McNeill
7. **Lionheart** Tommy Gemmell with Graham McColl
8. **A Season In Paradise** Henrik Larsson (with Mark Sylvester)
9. **A Bhoy's Own Story** Paul Lambert
10. **Scoring: An Expert's Guide** Frank McAvennie
11. **Celtic, My Team** Danny McGrain

YOU COULDN'T MAKE IT UP

11 farcical moments on and off the pitch

1. Send for a St Bernard

During a visit arranged by hosts Dynamo Zagreb prior to the 1963/64 European
Cup Winners' Cup clash, John Hughes and a wary John Divers decide to walk – rather
than take the cable car – down the 3,000ft Mount Sljeme. Bad move, lads. Marooned
after trying to take a shortcut, the pair are eventually rescued by police, driven

back to the top and then sent down in the cable car to be reunited with their team-mates. "You can imagine how popular we were when we got back on the bus," said Hughes. Oh yes, we can see it now.

2. Row, row, row your boat...
In May 1969 Jimmy Johnstone, having celebrated Scotland's home international win over Wales with a few drams, decides to cap a perfect night by walking along the shore at Largs. He is later rescued, singing to himself as he drifts out to sea, by the coastal authorities, having clambered into a rowing boat with just one oar.

3. I thought you said a ticket to Falkirk
May 1904 and 'Sunny' Jim Young finds himself stranded in Frankfurt station after misunderstanding instructions about a five-minute break before the train taking the players to Vienna leaves. Instead he'd taken 25 minutes, returning to find his team-mates gone. "If it hadnae been fur ma command o' languages" he claims he'd never have found them again.

4. Ciggies are no good for you
Right-back Jerry Reynolds leaves training with his team-mates McMahon and McCallum in July 1892. He pops into a tobacconist's. When he emerges he discovers they've left without him, for Nottingham and a fresh footballing start.

5. John, name your terms
The conversation between chief executive Allan MacDonald and John Barnes in 1999 which ends with Barnes accepting the offer to become head coach. If you ever had a go in a time machine, one of your first stops would surely be arriving at the start of this discussion and doing your utmost to stop it.

6. ...and a bottle of pop for the wee bairn
Roy Aitken, still 17, is required to report to the East German police so they can check he's being well looked-after as a minor before the Celts take on Sachsenring Zwickau in the 1976 Cup Winners' Cup quarter-final.

7. Have your prawn cocktail and I'll be back for the gateau
Sean Fallon signs Kenny Dalglish while out for a wedding anniversary meal with his wife and three daughters. Having asked them to wait a moment, he pops out and comes back two hours later.

8. Brolly good show
Kenny Dalglish's lost winner's medal from the 1977 Scottish Cup final turns up in

the umbrella of a man in a wheelchair he'd greeted after the match. Dalglish and Stein then mistakenly attempted to board the Rangers team bus, while holding the Cup. At least, that's their story...

9. Scrambled legs
The Celtic team spend the eve of the 1967 European Cup final watching the Spain v England friendly at the home of Scottish golfer Brodie Lennox, near their hotel. While walking back, trainer Neilly Mochan spots the hotel sign and the party clamber down the side of a hill in total darkness to take a short cut. "Anyone could have broken a leg," said Jim Craig.

10. Syme old Syme old
In the League Cup final of October 1986, referee Davie Syme is hit on the back by a coin. He mistakenly fingers Tony Shepherd and sends him off with two minutes left. When the error – another Syme classic – is pointed out, he calls him back on.

11. An inspector calls
In a separate incident in the same game, Syme also sent off Mo Johnston as the Old Firm clash threatened to get a bit too tasty. "Our players lost the place a wee bit," admitted manager Davie Hay. "The chief inspector came and told me that I needed to control them, but I ended up on the park with a ball. To this day, I don't know how."

ZIGGY STARDUST

Simple Minds front man Jim Kerr has always been Celtic daft. To find out which player he thought was "the next best thing to Ziggy Stardust", read on: here's his Celtic XI of personal favourites

1. Ronnie Simpson
No contest – it has to be the "auld yin".

2. Danny McGrain
Tough as nails. Hilariously, when he spoke in after-match interviews, no one could decipher a word he was saying.

3. Tommy Gemmell
The spitting image of Danny Kaye, but Big Tam almost burst the net in Lisbon.

4. Paul McStay
Wonderful player despite lacking the kind of arrogance that comes naturally to most Glaswegians.

5. Billy McNeill
Anyone nicknamed Caesar has a lot to live up to. A true Celtic captain, Billy ruled without having to watch his back.

6. Neil Lennon
The Northern Irishman takes immense stick from opposing fans in every game he plays. He's told me he loves it!

7. Jimmy Johnstone
Best winger ever. It was an honour for me to watch him set so many games on fire.

8. Kenny Dalglish
In 1973 he was the next best thing to Ziggy Stardust.

9. Henrik Larsson
Loved him, especially when he had his Genghis Khan moustache.

10. Charlie Nicholas
He was Bono in hoops!

11. Bobby Lennox
He never-ever stopped smiling, plus he was the fastest forward I have ever seen.